SEASONS

Poems of
Heartbreak, Hope, and Healing

by Marie Louise Andrews

SEASONS
Poems of
Heartbreak, Hope, and Healing
by Marie Louise Andrews

First Edition

ISBN: 978-0-9977147-5-3

With deep appreciation for those who devoted their time editing this book:
Kathleen Andrews, Eldon Baldwin, Nancy Bauer, Margaret Dunkle,
Russ and Martha Horton, Bobbie Patterson, and Barbara Sanders

Design by Suzanne Shelden

Photo and Artwork Credits are listed on pages 222 through 224

Published by:
Shelden Studios
PO Box 3221
Prince Frederick, Maryland 20678

Thank You

It is my great pleasure to express a joyful "Thank You" to each friend and supporter who provided the timely skill, support, and encouragement that assisted in the completion of this book:

Laura Adams

Dick Andrews

Jeffrey Andrews

Kathleen Andrews

Alyshia Bradley

Frannie Danvers

LeTia Dennison

Reverend Denise Diab

Liz Dombrovskis

Heather Donovan

Lydia Ford

Shawn Gantt

Rachel Garner

Wanda Granger

Ann Houpt

Bill Loftus

Carla Milling

Susan Wommack

Contents

✿

Winter

Spring

Summer

Fall

The Holidays

Welcome seekers, written word lovers, beauty devotees, human beings, learners, bereaved parents . . .

Looking back over almost a century of living, I realize how much my life has been personally influenced by war and the aftermath of war. I was born into a family whose maternal grandparents in Australia had received the news of the death of their son, Lieutenant Percy Binns, in France in the waning weeks of World War I. It preceded my birth by six years. My mother (his sister) and their distraught family were still mourning the "no-moreness" of their loved one.

I met my husband of seventy-five years when he was posted to Australia immediately after the United States entered World War II following Pearl Harbor. It is somewhat strange to feel grateful for this wartime meeting and marriage.

Then there came Vietnam when our Australian first-born child, John Michael Andrews, chose to volunteer in 1965 to become a helicopter pilot in the U.S. Army Air Corps. A crash caused his death and sent our Andrews family into a repeat of the 1918 tragedy.

One of my reactions was to join The Compassionate Friends Organization and I wrote a series of monthly poems from 1988 through 1995. This national organization provides support to bereaved parents whose child, or children, have died at all ages and from all causes.

The individual emotions, family changes, life style changes, and life-meaning questions experienced may also connect with facets of other types of loss, and may help family members and friends understand how they can relate more helpfully with their sorrowing loved one.

A new friend of mine whose adult son had died, and was herself a professor at a local college, told me that she had been given one of these poems and that it was the only thing she received that she found really helpful.

An African American father whose young adult son was murdered, received one of these Father's Day poems and responded: "I just wanted to let you know your poem, 'Father's Day,' meant a lot to me. It let me know that there are other people that lost their child and think and feel the same as myself. I could really relate to this poem."

A pastor who received two of these poems responded: "I must say, you write very well. I was struck most by your great imagery . . . you paint a scene so real that I can see it. Not only do I see the visual picture, but also feel the aching tenderness of loss. Both of your poems are very moving."

In retrospect, I realize that writing these poems was a form of therapy for me.

Cheers,
Marie Louise Andrews

SEASONS

Poems of
Heartbreak, Hope, and Healing

by Marie Louise Andrews

Winter

Remembering

We gather here . . .
To remember them . . .
Those ones so dear to us
Who fill our hearts with wonder, pain and joy.

For some,
That presence was as a 'field of dreams,'
   of expectations gone frightfully awry . . .
For some,
The knowledge of impending loss
   o'er many years . . .
For some,
The living that included anger, fear, despair . . .
For some,
The knock at the door,
   hearing those terrible words . . .
For some,
Watching the fast fall from health to death . . .

The circumstances differ,
The heart knows no such difference.

Only that great void . . .
   the empty chair,
   the not ringing of the phone,
   the no more of teasing and of laughter,
     the soul,
       that seeks meaning
        from such madness.

For all, the time was far too short . . .
And now, what do we do with our present time?

At first, survival is the task.
Each day, each hour, each minute,
How to support the siblings,
How to support our partners in their grief,
For those now alone, how to support
    that self in such aloneness?

Each present here today
    is a winner, of many
    battles deep within,
There is a pool of common
    understanding here today
That arises from hard journeys travelled,
    on roads so rough and desolate.

Yet here we are today,
Surviving the journey,
Knowing life more truly,
Knowing ourselves more deeply,
Living our lives in ways not
    formerly dreamed of . . . living!

We hold the memories of our child,
   our children, close,
We add the learnings
   that the months and years have wrought
We now live our lives
   melded with the being of our child,
And find a richness there,
And look for ways to share
   this melding of loved lives
In new ways . . .
   in our own lives . . .
   in our ongoing relationships
   in our interactions in the world . . .

As we ponder anew the depths of LOVE!

New Year 1995

What shall I do with this old year
Now coming to a close?
That's been so full of pain and turmoil,
This first year of the death of my child?

Will this grayness, this
   sadness, then leave me?
I know now, it's not tuned to
   change of year.
Yet there's a niggling thought.
   that turning this year's page
Somehow makes the separation
   more final.

What shall I do with New Year's Eve
midst the parties and the celebrations,
when the ball descends at midnight,
when the bell has tolled this year
     for my loved child?

Another step on this long journey,
that in nightmare I could n'er imagine.
Yet a walk through what must be walked,
   'long the road to new tomorrow.

For those who look back o'er the years,
the old intensity, remembered, and now gone,
    there linger still
      unanswerable questions,
how would it be now,
     if my child had lived?

As I make my list at New Years,
it seems that feelings,
         not resolutions, are the core,
to honestly acknowledge . . .
anger, fear, sadness, guilt,
         emptiness, resentment,
the fierce wanting of my child,
         yet knowing that it cannot be.

Slipping into the New Year,
it comes, ready or not,
taking each day gently,
caring for what I've still got.

Myself . . . the ones I love . . .
my skills . . . my heart expanded . . .
sharing all that is uniquely me
with others, on their own new journey.

I discover that I've learned and grown
in ways formerly not known,
my child, nestled within, in a new way,
has taught me things unimaginable,
and now lives on within my heart,
together into New Year 1995.
We'll walk into this new time coming . . .
into this world . . . with Love!

Moving Ahead

How can I wish for the New Year
when my heart is claimed by the old,
by the wish that cannot be granted,
the life that is still and cold?

Let my love go out to that mem'ry,
of the times of sorrow and joy;
and a thankfulness fill in my being
that the life that I loved so, was lived.

Now, I wish that the sorrow will lessen,
and I work through the days of my grief,
while a Love surrounds and supports me
though the mind searches long for belief.

My wish is to know more than Love
both to receive and to give,
by sharing my love with all others
I'll more surely know I now live!

Let's wish all together this New Year
that our mem'ries bring joy more than pain;
let's share with all others our learnings,
let's find our living, our gain.

Loss . . . Rebirth

Now comes the season of bare branches,
and on the bare, brown ground
        all ridges etched,
the valleys and the hills show starkly:
elemental form unfolds.

My life stands so exposed these days.
I see what formerly was covered.
The different shape of things;
the bones now bare.

The landscape of my life in these hard days
is sharply hewn and solitary.
I gaze at things not seen before:
the bedrock of my soul.

The pruner's heavy hand has wrought
a shape for me that alien feels,
and I must readjust my being
to not be overcome by terror.

In this bare season then
I will commune within,
to touch deep wellsprings there
with waters now awaiting for release.

Slowly, slowly, the waters flow,
at first an oozing midst the mud,
a lessening of the parchedness,
some small movement out of barrenness.

One day, along the path a touch of green,
the next a snowdrop blooms
amidst the old dried leaves,
amidst the ice-encrusted snow.

I gaze and gaze,
the tears drop silently,
then sudden sobs engulf me,
as I give thanks for hope anew.

And within, a knowledge slowly grows,
that these hard pruned branches of my life
will too, some day, leaf out again,
to gain a shape more fitting this new season.

And once more there will be buds, then flowers;
a new beauty and new bounty
born of this hard pruning,
a season of new fruit will come again.

So let the bells of New Year ring.
The season of renewal of my soul shall bring
a deeper understanding of communion.
Ring out the old, ring in the new,
may their joint ringing bring
a melody of peace within.

New Year's Path

On this day . . . .
 it is the New Year!
 a new year after the death of my child.

I look out and see
 the sand, swept clear by the tide
 no footprints on its smooth
 washed surface;
 the woods, now bare of summer's thicket
 with silhouettes of trunk and limb
 outlined against the brilliant sky;
 the land, white sheeted with new fallen
 snow that tucks the plants
 into the earth.

Everything reduced to its minimum.
Only the changeless changing of the season;
Only the dependability of fall and re-birth.
Only the ceaseless caring of the universe
 for its earth child.

And what of my child's . . . now absence?
and of a parent's caring?
and of a parent's . . . . . . now living?

I understand now through my grieving more . . .
    the stripped down form of things
    the actions that matter
    the values that matter.
From the bowels of my sorrow
    there emerges from the darkness
a vision more true to love
    than any known before
a heart more tender now
    than any known before.

And now this living
    incorporates
        in some new born way
all the understandings of my love
    for my child
and the knowledge and the lessons
    of all our times together
and the knowledge and the lessons
    of that life now gone beyond . . .
and the thoughts of what my child
    would now for me be wanting . . .

And now I see a pathway
    in the snow
    or sand
    or through the woods
that follows more the dictates of
    a tear-scarred heart!
and seeks beauty born of all now known
and seeks a path into the year ahead
where love and gentleness and peace is fed.

What Will I Do with the 'New Year?'

The old year dies . . .
but I am still glued to it!
In this first year after your death,
   my child,
   I cannot let go . . .
   cannot let go of my
      need for you,
   cannot let go of these
      overwhelming feelings,
   cannot let go of your
      no longer being with me . . .
and so I cling to the old year
yet know that the New Year is here.

It seems sometimes
   a travesty, a disloyalty
      to your being,
      to our love,
   to step into this New Year.
How can I resolve these thoughts?

How to move forward?
   Yet keep close my love for you?
How to let go of you?
   Yet to keep you in my heart always?

This is the turmoil of my days,
   and my nights;
This is the confusion that
   binds tight my mind.

Can it be true, as someone said,
    that as I let go
    the memories will start to flow?
    that as I accept the loss
    there can truly be a gain?
What does it take
    to take such a chance?

Some will say that it takes
    weeks, months, maybe years
        of trying all other ways
        to assuage this loss,
of finding that these ways don't work,
        of bottoming out . . .
                no place else to go . . .

Before it is possible
    to just . . . let . . . go,
    to just . . . let . . . be.

And sometimes, surprisingly,
    into this sad, dry place
    will flow a spring of hope,
    will flow new memories of our child
        that light a flame . . .
    will flow an energy
        built of those memories
            of our child;
        built of our love
            for our child.

And now we might know an
  overwhelming thankfulness
      for the life of our child . . .
entwined in a new way within us,
and celebrate that love that
    warms our heart anew.

And now,
  let us step forth
      in the New Year of 1992 . . .
sometimes still sad . . .
sometimes very tentatively . . .
sometimes, miraculously,
    with enthusiasm . . .

Always with a deep knowing
that there is hope
    in this New Year!

New Year's Promise

What will I do with the New Year
when my heart lies heavy and cold,
when ice and snow cover the outside,
and inside, my chest a dull load?

The child of my loins is not with me
and I dwell on that loss day and night.
Will a time ever come here within me
when I'll let go of the terrible weight?

If my child knew of this sadness and longing,
I wonder what words would be said?
Could be: "Loved ones, get on with your living,
You have so much still to be giving."

"The love that has been there between us
e'en the anger, disappointment, some hate,
are all part of what happens between us,
who live on this earth and who mate."

It's the love that shines through in the morning,
the hope that rises up like a flame
that fills this cold heart with a warming,
for life is both changed, yet the same.

I will never be like I was yesterday
your spirit has mingled with mine
a new love that's born of this suffering
brings a peace which is surely the sign!

So in this New Year that's here now
your presence within me abides
and slowly the pain turns to fullness
as thankfulness flows like the tides.

Ringing in the New Year

The Old Year endeth.

For one whose grief is fresh,
    the thoughts can bring on panic.
I'm not yet ready to relinquish
    the closeness of the present year.
It makes the 'never seeing you again'
    become too real.
No . . . I can only hear
    the tolling of the bell this year.

Sometimes along this journey,
    new feelings and new thoughts arise.
It's still hard to let the years slip by.
Yet more grieving has been done
    and the reality of loss accepted more.
Beyond the hurt and pain arises,
    on occasion, a flame of hope,
    that this year coming round,
    may be better than the last.
My child's memories now come forth
    without the unceasing anguish
    of former years.
In some way the ringing of the bells
    moves my sad heart into the future.

For those whose mourning almost seems
    an old and well known friend,
    that greatest loss is somehow now
        part of life on-going . . .
            acquainted with the still sharp
            stabs of unexpected memory.
You are always there,
    and precious in my heart.
Your living and your dying
    have changed me in ways unmeasurable . . .

How can a parent possibly accept the gift
    of life's learning from a child who died?
Yet in some unfathomable way
    that is the gift my child has given.

So when the bells ring out,
    I'll stand in silence and in wonder,
    at what my child has wrought . . .

Those chimes, sounding
        on that New Year's night,
    and ringing to the farthest shining star,
        become the music of the spheres
            that meld my love
                with Love Eternal.

Cold Heart . . . Warm Heart

A heart lies cold
a heart feels dead,
how can it flutter on
when my child is dead?

A heart flutters on
beyond all belief,
what keeps it going
there is no relief.

The weeks go by
it all seems so gray,
the loss of my child
is here to stay.

The months go by
some warmth returns,
as friends prove that love
can never be spurned

The first year goes by
my heart cries out,
that the love of my child
lives on without doubt.

It lives on in my heart
and it turns into the deeds
before never possible.
My child planted the seeds.

Now my heart knows
both the cold and the warmth
as our lives intermingle
is unexpected . . . . new birth!

A Heart Weeps

Today, from that barren earth
A clump of green appeared
White snowdrops, clustered there.
White snowdrops, clustered in the green
   And I saw, once again, a fragment of beauty!

I weep with thanksgiving
For this beauty that has warmed me.
For this heart that leapt, and now knows
That joy can enter once again.

This is a level of loss
That numbs every part of my being
My heart is bound so tightly
That it cannot weep.
   Will this time ever end?

The ground lies bare and brown
Covered with last year's leaves.
The earth is cold and hard
As desolate as my heart.
   Sustain me in this hour!

A Quickened Heart

These days are bone-chill cold.
The rocks along the Bay shore
look sugar coated, but
I know it is ice out there.

Tree limbs are silhouetted
against the dull grey clouds,
torn limbs and scarred knots
exposed to vicious winds.

This bleak outer landscape
mirrors my own inner one.
In these endless days
after the death of my child.

In this heart bereft time
so much is cold and lonely;
so much is pain and loss.
This new terrain seems bottomless!

It hurts to hear the season's music
of hearts entwined and glowing.
Red hearts are everywhere!
And mine own lies bleeding.

Oh yes, I know of love . . .
Remember days that used to be,
together in our joy and innocence;
together, building memories.

Each year, the cards are on the shelves.
Each year the pain cuts deep.
Each year there are the ones
    who care and comfort me.

And slowly, as the years go by,
those acts of love draw out
a new response from my sad heart;
a thawing of that coldness.

Slowly, I feel hope again.
Slowly, a new love arises.
Slowly, I can give again,
    from a healing heart.

I always will remember
    the ones who stood by me
    in my time of sorrow.
They, I hold most dear.

And now their gift of Love to me,
    is mine anew to share
        with others who are hurt and sad
        who need another's care

And in this deeper knowledge,
    born of loss, of grief, of love,
    lives my child whose life and death
    occasioned agony and thankfulness.

A gratitude, so slowly understood,
    for all that life has given,
        and for my child.
Who now lives on
    within my quickened heart!

Early Morning Walk

In the first light, over the Bay,
    wind slaps waves to white froth
        on the wild water;
On land, trees twist tumultuously
    as leaves lash limbs to the breaking point . . .
    echoing the confusion in my mind
    in those days,
    after the death of my child.

Up from the water,
    gold against a rosy sky,
        shoots the sun
        with fierce beauty,
too overwhelming to my dulled eyes.
I must turn in self-protection
I cannot yet receive
    that ravishing hope
    so soon . . . .
    after the death of my child.

Walking inland,
    the moon still gleams in
        inscrutable paleness
           in the lightening sky . . .

Yet there is a certainty
　　to its appearance, its disappearance,
　　its changing shapes,
　　its altering tides;
　　a familiarity, a reassurance,
　　　　that order still exists . . . .
My mind in these days
　　needs to clutch for
　　　　some semblance of orderliness.

Further inland,
　　branches lie along the pathway,
　　a great tree has fallen on the road,
　　its offending trunk cut by a chain saw
　　　　to clear the way . . . . .
My heart feels the cut of its blade
　　in this grieving time.

A pond gleams silently along my way,
　　its waters calm.
　　　　a small splashing release of water
　　　　　　at one place on the bank
　　　　　　assures a constant level.
Reflection of now still trees
　　balances quietly a former tumult.
　　　　When will my heart be done with tumult?
　　　　When will my mind know spreading calm?

The walk goes on,
    day after day,
    month after month,
    year after year.

The sun shines high,
waves on the Bay now light.
Water shines and sparkles in the sun's rays.
In other places, bright blue is everywhere.
I feed now on this beauty,
    and am not overcome,
        wildness and terror have calmed,
        they have endured.

My child's life has moved on . . .
I remain,
    to share the beauty, the sometimes despair,
    to do my best, for he would care . . .
    that his living,
        may go on living
    through my hands and heart
I dare . . .
    to hold the goodness of the world,
    and to move it forward . . .
        in his name!

The Season of the Heart

This is the Season of the Heart! Yet many of us
will be asking how to live during this season
with a heart that is broken. Just what is it that
our hearts are knowing during these days?
What are the feelings that pulsate and ebb and
flow? Is it . . .

> the Heart that catches its breath on a
>   memory and is overwhelmed?
> the Heart that feels it absolutely cannot
>   hold one more ounce of pain?
> the Heart that knows the fleeting smile
>   of a loved one?
> the Heart that catches a fragment of joy
>   and is warmed?
> the Heart that is tempted
>   to lie still and lonely?
> the Heart that searches for
>   the acceptance of a friend?
> the Heart that one day,
>   suddenly, surprisingly knows joy!

Questions arise! Why is a heart red and why
does it have two lobes? A response might be . . .

> A heart is so vulnerable; so easily bloodied.
> A heart consists of opposites;
>   changed by sorrow and by joy.
> A heart, when whole, includes all emotions
> A heart can lie cold and sad and broken . . .
> A heart can grow and heal and love . . .

We each have our own choice to make!

A Heart of Love

Down by the Bay,
The scene is monochrome.
Shades of grey exist.
Shades of grey exist within my heart.

This winter of my discontent goes on,
How long? How long?
Yet sometimes newness enters in,
and I can choose to let it flourish or decay.

This life, that sometimes now
seems less than half a life,
is what I have received . . .
to respond to as I choose.

Even midst the sadness and the loss
My heart is beating, albeit thumping often!
What is the course I'll set my life upon,
After the death of my child?

Slowly moves my mind and heart,
listening to impulses from within,
from those regions comes a stirring
of life, now seeking new expression.

Will I allow new life to rise,
From the ashes of my grief,
and play and dance to music faintly heard,
and let new wonder sing?

Now I see beyond the gray
Red, bright is everywhere,
and shapes of hearts,
and love songs in the air!

Oh love, once torn asunder,
Now brightens and exults these days,
Love of child now gone before . . .
Leads me to embrace life's love again!

Oh Love, that will not let me go,
I'll claim my place again on earth's abode,
and once again, within the Cosmos,
I feel Creation's Love upholding me!

Red Heart

Red hearts are everywhere:
They stretch for what seems miles
   along the card displays,
they're on teddy bears,
   on bags and boxes,
   in the candy stores,
   the advertisements.

Each time they overwhelm me . . .
They speak of love, of gaiety,
   of what is normal . . .
they speak of hugs and smiles,
   of expectations of happiness . . .

They slap me up, straight and cold.
They rush anguish
   to my chest and throat
   in tight, constricting hands,
they bring the "no more-ness"
   of this time
before my dull glazed eyes.
I want to run away forever;
I would if I had the energy!
I want to hide and never be seen,
But, oh, it is so lonely there!

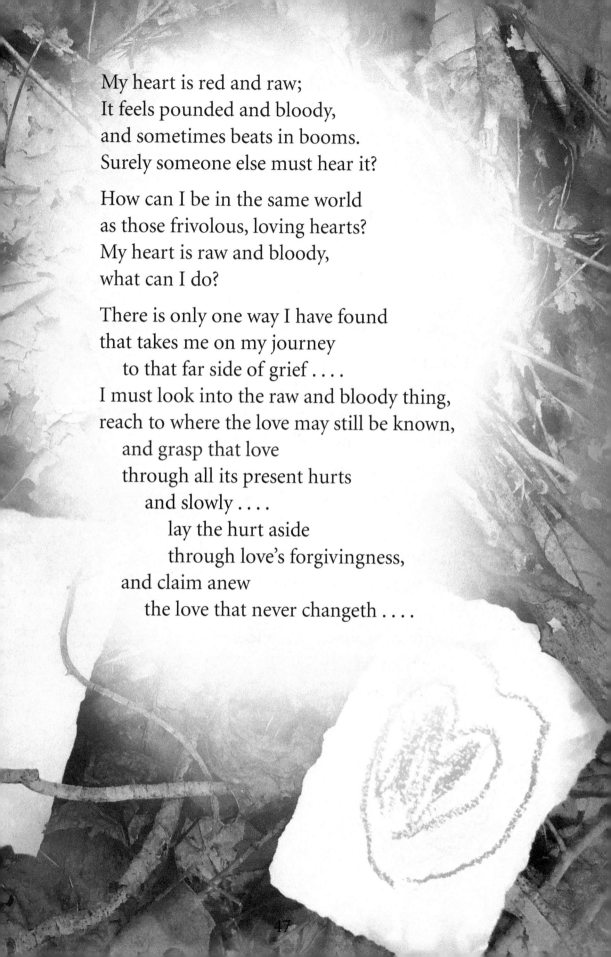

My heart is red and raw;
It feels pounded and bloody,
and sometimes beats in booms.
Surely someone else must hear it?

How can I be in the same world
as those frivolous, loving hearts?
My heart is raw and bloody,
what can I do?

There is only one way I have found
that takes me on my journey
    to that far side of grief . . . .
I must look into the raw and bloody thing,
reach to where the love may still be known,
    and grasp that love
    through all its present hurts
      and slowly . . . .
        lay the hurt aside
        through love's forgivingness,
   and claim anew
        the love that never changeth . . . .

The love first known in parenthood,
   the love that wells within
   while looking at one's sleeping child,
   the love that answers to the loved child's
          needs . . .
   the love that now needs
      to turn full circle
      and lovingly fulfill
          on our own life's needs,
      a love that can forgive our own misdeeds.

That Love beyond our own
   that pulses through our bodies
      from both near and far . . . .
from realms where all is Love . . . .
   to seek and find
          its place of peace and hope
          within our heart.

That once again our heart
   may know a wholeness
      in a new way
      of profound reverence
   for the mystery
      of Love.

Between Us
Bereaved Fathers and Mothers

My heart lies heavy this morning.
How can I drag myself through this day?
I will just sit here
   in this screaming grayness
   and feel the tightness
     in my throat
     and across my chest
     and in my gut.

My heart lies heavy this morning.
But I must get out, to work.
I almost hit that car along the Beltway!
I must not let my thoughts slip away . . .
   to lie with my child who is dead.

Maybe I'll phone my friend
She/he listens to me, better than anyone else.
I need, so much, someone who will listen,
   who will understand.
I can no longer continue saying the same
   things, over and over again, to my mate.
I've realized he/she doesn't really want
   to hear me anymore,
And I wonder,
   'Did I love our dead child more?'
   and a great anger comes over me,
   and a great sadness comes over me,
   for I am so alone.

And I wonder what answers I will discover,
And I wonder what actions I will choose,
As I lie
    with my loved one who hurts
As I lie
    hurting in the long night hours.

And I search for ways to be more understanding
To listen once more, and again . . .
                            one more time,
To reach out and share my grief with my love,
To reach out and be tender with my love,
To reach out and say the loving word
                            to my love,
To reach out and hold tight . . . . . to my love.

I'll keep so busy
    that there is no second of time
    for those painful thoughts to enter.
I'll work, work, work ! ! !
Yet I'm not very productive
    even in my over-working.
There is so much confusion
    and my mind just darts
        unheedingly, and
        seemingly unendingly,
        here, there everywhere.

Do I really want to come home
    to those hurting eyes
    and those hard sobs?
    to that overwhelming sadness?

Can I get away from all this pain
   by running away
     and never returning?
   by finding a new mate
     who does not have those hurting eyes?

Maybe I'll sleep tonight
   if I have that extra drink
   or take that second pill.
Those nights, when I'm awake
   and remember . . . .
   I feel consumed by my despair.

To remember the early days
      of our love for each other
To remember our wonderment
      at the life of our child
To remember the joys and the sadness
      we have known together

So that the present differences in grieving
   can be accepted,
the present hurts
   can be heard,
the present angers
   can be tolerated,
the present aloneness
   can be endured.

For this is the path of grief.
So much longer, and harder, and more painful
    than we could ever have imagined.
So much more to be gained for living,
    and for each other,
        when we stay the course.

May we find
    that small glimmer of extra energy,
        to reach out,
    that heart that lightens as forgiveness
        allows us to let go of anger,
    that hope that allows me to respond tenderly
        to our intuition, gently leading,
    that love is rekindled,
        and warms,
        and grows, once more,
        BETWEEN US!

        . . . closure.

Shadow, Sun, and Soul

This winter has been harsh:
a cold of record lows,
ice storms of record damage,
for some, no water, heat, or electricity.

To live, deep in the root of things,
to find a way through darkness,
to find some light amid that darkness,
to find the core, and learn to live in it.

Beyond this whiplash of the season,
those of whose child has died
uncover soon another depth
within our mind, our heart, our soul.

We wander in this alien place,
sometimes mute,
sometimes with great wailing,
for this loss of one so loved,
for this unknown, and
uncomprehended, time.

Walking a way not dreamed of,
seeking a path that moves the stone
from heart and soul,
that slowly allows
a new vision to unfold . . .

Thoughts and feelings,
overwhelming and confused . . .
   of anger, betrayal, resentment
   of guilt, sadness, rejection,
   of love, tenderness, wonder
   of love, love, love . . .

We need to think our thoughts
of how our lives have been,
acknowledge all our present pain,
reflection on the memories so dear,
placing them within our soul,
to enrich and recreate our present life . . .

As new green shoots emerge from icy shadows
wonder how seed, earth,
   and darkness each together
create this growing greenness;
may our spirit resurrect . . . .
   from our own deep journey,
   and bring forth new flowers,
   from what we thought was wasteland.
   from what we come to understand . . . .
     as life's journey . . . .
     a journey of the soul . . . .

The Healing Journey

In this early time, for those
    so newly bereft,
        the long slow passage of
        the hours and days,
            is what is known.

In this time,
    for some; there is a slow,
    slow lessening of the pain
    and hurt.

In this time,
    for others, there is a
    deeper knowledge that this
    loss is so great
    it can be integrated into our
    life ongoing.

                  In this time
    for others who have walked
    the lonely path of grief,
    the memory of our child has
      melded,
    into a heart once saddened,
    that now beats to a deeper song,
by love renewed and now
    sent forth,
    from an integration of the
    living of that much loved child,
    and all the wounding,
    healing things now learnt,
now bursts forth into a wounded healer;

From this shattered, wounded,
    healing heart comes grateful thanks,
for the living of that life so precious,
and to the spirit that
    engendered hope again,

And now the soul sings through
    that force of love
and shines unblinking
    into the depth of all.

Spring

Along the Way

There is this small place
    my heart now inhabits.
I sometimes feel entombed
    myself by grief.

Where formerly I flew
    on wings of light
and knew no boundaries
    that grabbed and held me tight . . .
      Now all has changed.

I plod painfully along
    each hour, each day,
    each month, each year,
A minefield is out there it seems
    to shatter in a thousand
    unsuspected ways,
      Yet still I live.

"What for?" "What for?"
    my heart cries out,
and deep within I know
    that I must search
    and answer that hard need.

Sometimes the answer comes
    in one swift burst of knowing;
Sometimes it is the
    slow accumulation
    of the days and nights of grief
that opens through the clouds
    a sudden ray of light
and one more thing is
    then resolved
along the winding road.

It may be so many things . . .
    the unexpected kindness,
    the sharing of a gnawing
        feeling with a friend.

The sudden seeing once again
        of beauty . . .
    in a flower,
    in the wind in the long grass,
    in the trusting smile of a child
    in tenderness of an arm
        around a shoulder,
    in the friend who continues
        to call and 'be' there
    in the beauty of another heart
        that has been wounded.

When the spirit of compassion
    and of love
    explodes the bitter mines
        of isolation or of guilt
        or of any other hurt
and once again allows the heart
    to open and expand
    and slowly to absorb
        once more
    the beauty and wonder of it all.

That shriveled, hard-held heart
    can now grow soft;
    can now know healing;
    can now speak the words,
    "I now know Hope!"

It may be just a moment . . .
    but that moment has occurred.
Imprinted now in memory
    to be recalled at will.

At the deepest
        level of my soul
Hope has re-imprinted!
Thanksgiving overflows!

My child's life lives on in me,
And speaks the words of
        love,
And speaks the words of
        newness and renewal.

For now our lives
are intertwined
        in memory,
        and in my acts;
Engendered by
        new understandings
                so reverently . . .
                so passionately . . .
                        received.

Springtime

Now comes the time when spring is
    bursting out all over.
The sun comes early and stays late.
Flowers bloom, and birds sing sweetly.
Oh, the beauty of it all!
Oh the searing pain of it
    to those whose grief is fresh.

So much has changed!
The innocence of former days
When life itself seemed endless,
When there was time unquestioned,

When days flowed by with minor
    mishaps.

Old assumptions now lie shattered,
Old relationships are changed.
Emotions cause a certain craziness.
The very core of self is rent.

My child . . . my children . . .
This hole within my heart and life
Feels like nothing I have known before.

Where will I start
To pull together all these
    broken strands?
For I must start, I know that now.
Yet only slowly rises strength
    for new beginnings.

At first I need to acknowledge to
    myself, this pain and hurt
And later bring to mind
The thousand things you meant
    to me.
Counting all of them as gain.
Thankful for your presence here.

Remembering . . . remembering . . .
    The sweetness of your being here.
    The learning that encounter gave.

Then to place in sacred memory
    the heart of you,
that now must beat within my heart.

Your life will now be known
    within my own,
The hopes, the dreams,
    the presence of you,
Now will bring new
    understandings to my own.

My child . . . my children . . .
Now embraced within my heart.
A strange, undreamed of . . .
    resurrection,
on the road of life eternal.

Dawn

The night has been filled with
restlessness;
a heart pounding in panic
a throat clutched dry
the visual memories the mind
attempts to reject
of that one day,
the thoughts that crowd in confusion
the tears that flow, or refuse to flow.

In the first light
there is only silhouette
black upon grey
the starkness of it tears apart
the fog of the night
the cutting edges of it
pains all my being.

In the east
one strip of pink shines between
grey water and the overcast.
A moment of color, of beauty,
that my heart can scarcely accept
before the clouds move across again.

Yet my heart has been moved by that beauty.
There is now a hope
There is now a thankfulness
	for the message that comes
When my mind centers on
	that pink glow!

Later . . .
	colors return in their intensity,
And I remember
I have known the dark, the grey, the bright
	new dimensions of life
	new windows of values
	new clarity that illuminates.

Yet always,
	again and again,
	the remembrance of that first pink glow,
		so brief,
		bringing a deep thankfulness
that dawn will come!

Old Print

It hangs upon my wall.
A copy of a drawing,
    taken many years ago;
    and old newspaper print titled:
"Decoration Day, 1881."

The old man, kind and wise
    seated on a low stone wall . . .
The children, with their school slates
    and wide open eyes,
    stop to stare and listen
        as he points beyond the wall
            to silent markers on the ground,
            beside the silent church.

I wonder what his words convey;
What events have filled his life
    as he speaks to those young children,
    as he explains the meaning of the scene.
Do his sons or daughters lie
    beneath the stones on that
        still hillside?

What other hearts held close to bursting
    from a grief for young ones lost?
How can that scene of quiet reverence,
of new generations learning of such loss,
    from such a tender man
Be ever reconciled with that wild beating
    in my heart:
With that cold sadness in my memory?

I waken, on this day,
   to a world of grey,
   with clouds above and silver on the Bay.
   And in the east, a golden window
      open from above
      as rays of sun pour down
         from parted clouds
      to form within a space 'tween
         cloud and sea
      a golden scene of beauty
         and amazement.
And I am silent with the wonder of it all,
And give thanks for all that
   was, and is, and will be . . .

For memories, through the pain,
   that bring glad thoughts of days gone by
      when all was well;
For present wonders that invade my heart
   with unexpected joy:
For newborn hope that holds together
   what has been
   and bids me move ahead
   and bids me be that wiser one
      who sits now, myself,
      on old stone walls
And speaks with children of new generations.

My heart whispers longingly . . .
   Let this come to be!

On Finding a Light

These days are very hard,
The world seems grey,
enshrouded in fog;
pain stabs at my heart,
or twists my gut;
confusion confounds
and distorts all my thoughts.
. . . and joy is absent,
completely unknown.

There is this longing
to know again
that which can be no more;
there is this sense of stagnation,
a lack of energy,
or sometimes,
a frightening wildness,
I am in unchartered territory,
a body with strange symptoms
a mind that feels mindless.
In this unknown landscape
there is isolation . . .
    Numbness . . . a void.

They say I should be getting over it by now.
My friends, caring,
yet uncomfortable with grief.
I say, "I too, wish it were so,
but that just is not the way it really is."

One day, amidst the darkness
I heard another speak of loss and pain
My heart went out to meet that other heart . . .
and suddenly, surprisingly, momentarily,
my heart lit up!

It seemed such a small event
on one level
yet I knew . . . that all had changed,
for one short moment I had fled
the darkness and the aloneness of my grief.
I had discovered that
new love still lay within my heart
and that love could light the darkness
for it now understood another's pain.

I had discovered that in reaching out
there was a fullness in my heart again.
There was warmth instead of that dark coldness.
There was this moment of healing,
between my own heart and another's.

O Light that comes in every darkness
though so small and weak at first
ignite the dullness in my soul
that healing love may now illumine me.

May Love then touch each thought
and action that I take
and Peace of starlit skies enfold my heart
as thoughts of times both past and present
are woven strand by strand . . .
                    in loving memory.

On Father's Day

I often wonder . . .
Thinking of the fathers and their grief . . .
At the hurt that lingers in their eyes,
And almost see the dreams that
   have been shattered,
Even when no words are ever spoken.

I often wonder . . .
Where and how that hurt dissolves . . .
   into anger, wild and dangerous . . .
   into resentment, eroding all so slowly . . .
   into the physical, of pain and lost immunity.

I often wonder . . .
How to coax from tight-bound places
All those thoughts that linger there . . .
   the *if only's* that so haunt the mind . . .
   the *why's* of such unfairness . . .
   the wishes that an action could be undone,
     or, could still be done . . .

I often wonder . . .
How those feelings that lie covered
might be allowed to be expressed,
   in healing ways . . .
     in words with another who accepts . . .
   in thoughts expressed in
     writings that disclose . . .
   in swift release on playing field . . .
   in the roar of confrontation with that one,
   in the silence of deep communion with that one.

And I am grateful . . .
    for the fathers of those
    children who have died.

I see . . .
      the pain.
    and know that love is there,
      and know that love will never die.
I see . . .
    the searching,
      for what must be done to live again . . .
    to do mourning that alone
      allows new life to flow . . .
    to bring the memories,
      at first so painful,
    into recognition and accept
Until, at last, the memories bring pleasure,
Until, at last, the hurt turns into healing.

Your way of searching and of healing,
May be very different from my own, dear one.
At first, that can be hard to understand.
Yet that understanding
    is of great importance . . .
It is our gift of acceptance,
    of continuing on together,
      of deepest love,
        to each other!

Rain

It rained, rained, rained,
    echoing the tears in my heart.
The potholes filled with water,
    it lay in the ditches
    and across the fields,
Everything was waterlogged,
    Until the sun came . . .
    and then I noticed . . .
        that in some places
        where the mud had been cracked
        and dust blew across
        the now-parched earth.

But in other places . . .
Where the ground lay covered
    with rich humus
    of last year's leaves
    or the growth of seeds
    from the dark . . .
That now the grass grew green
    and the beauty of wild flowers
        sprang from the decay.

Oh that my heart may be born anew
    from the seed bed of life!
Oh that my soul may blossom once again
    from the dark decay of my loss!

Green and Gold

A whorl of slender green
where yesterday was none,
and from its center shone
a small golden-throated flower.

Down on my knees
and leaning low,
exploring this exploding beauty,
bright shining as new-risen sun
upon the waters of the Bay.

Pulsations of shimmering
    light and warmth
    energy and life
drew me inward,
infusing all within that glow.

In that unexpected, startling beauty
    the darkness
    the tightness
    the despair
were gone.

Only my heart
    beating in tune with that beauty
    beating the sense of the warmth
    beating the desire of that wonder once again!

Out of the earth bare and hard borne
    from the loss and the pain
    born of weeks, months, years, of such sadness
opened my heart once again.

When Will I Ever Learn?

When will I ever LEARN ...?
   in these terrible first days and months
   after the death of my child ...
that those light footsteps will not return,
that that laugh will no longer be heard,
that the "Hi Mom" "Hi Dad"
     will now be silent ...
   silent as my hurting heavy heart.

How can I ever learn
   to accept this loss of my flesh
   this child of my womb or my sperm?
It seems an impossible nightmare,
Yet walking, the death is still there.

Why has this dreadful thing happened?
   to me, to us, to my family?
   Why has this come to pass,
     in the scheme of things ...?

When will I ever FEEL again ...
   the glow of living in this world?
So many days
   it all seems dull and void,
   a black hole without end.
How will I ever feel again
   the normal joys once known before?

It seems impossible
    to even consider
        laughter, joy and beauty,
How can the sun shine its daily round
    midst my whirling confusion of feelings;
        such sadness, pain, anger, guilt or hate?

When will I ever KNOW
    the feelings that the wise ones spoke of?
        the 'peace that passeth understanding.'

Oh, let me feel again . . .
    the beauty of this world . . .
    the deep stirrings of compassion . . .
    the love that encompasses and heals . . .
    the serenity of life with meaning . . .
    that 'peace that passeth understanding.'

In my heart I know this is what my child
    would want for me.

May I have the courage to walk the path
    toward this place!

Cycles

Looking into the woods
   and over the bare ground
   in these days before the leaves grow
I see the form of things not seen before . . .
   the sloping outline of the gully,
   the shape of trees both small and large,
   the texture of their trunks and limbs
     now stand revealed.

Soon, the lines of land and trunks of trees
   will show again no more
   as spring brings forth its flowers
     and its leaves
   to perfume and enclose
   the starkness of pure form;
And senses gather voluptuously
   in the riot of such fullness
And hearts know once again
   the increase of the days.

While in my life
   the time now tastes of winter
   and I would bid it pass into a spring.
Yet never will the forms of that cold time
   slip completely out of memory
For things now known because my child
    has died
   will dwell forever in a new known place

And outlines of that time when truth lay hard
    upon a soul bereft
will always be within this life now stirring;
a wild, momentous knowledge
    of the sting of grief
    that intermingles always with my life.

And as the blossoms sing of newness
        once again,
    and open full of beauty and of bounty,
I know, too, that blossom-fall will come
    as the cycle moves into completion.

I know, too, to sing a song to beauty . . .
To name the name who can no longer sing . . .
To live a life wherein dwells
    all that has been . . .

So that love and pain and beauty walk
    together in my heart
To light the path that stretches out ahead!

Awakening

This child of mine . . .
    who filled my days with laughter
    sometimes filled my days with tears
      will now never act again for joy or woe . . .
Yet I must act. But how?

Every thought and action now seems frozen
mid the pain of loss and sorrow
dreams and hopes of yesterday are only
ashes still hot red with hurting.

When all the earth is greening once again
sun rises early on the bay, and flowers bloom
what can be done with anguish such as this
each hour and day the yearning tugs my
    heart anew.

This must be so, how less could be the grief
for such a loss as this?
Mind, body, soul must weep . . .
before new dawning comes.

Slowly, slowly, comes a glimmer . . .
    blossoms on still dark tree branches,
    bird song enters into consciousness,
    scent of rose geraniums in sunny spaces,
    eyes that meet in understanding,
    hearts that listen to my halting words,
    arms that silently enfold with love;
and pieces of the pain are loosened,
hope flutters for a moment,
    a heart gives thanks.

Slowly, slowly, over and over,
    responses to beauty and love
    bring light strokes of awakening to my soul.

Slowly, slowly, over and over,
    one more small piece of pain is laid aside
    and from the memory that once hurt so hard
    arises now remembrance of the joys we shared.

I begin to understand the ways of grief . . .
The valley that my feet are walking now
    leads some place that was formerly
        undreamed of:
A deeper, higher, inter . . . union
    with
        all being.

And now I know that a grief hard walked
    gives pain a purpose
        in a hurting world,
and my child's life lives on within my own
    as aching tenderness,
        that wakens healing
        in another's heart.

New Bouquet

I watched that bud
   all winter long . . .
   at first so small and slender
   nestled in green shiny leaves.

As winter waned
   it continued to swell
   a promise of life enripening.
And I remembered the ways
   and hopes of pregnancy.

And then the green bud split
   and a whiteness
   forced open from its center,
   disclosing, so slowly,
   the beauty and delicacy
   of its petaled blossom.

And I remembered the time of birth
   and the days and the years of unfolding.

Some buds dropped unopened to the earth
   their beauty only guessed at . . .
Some buds, barely opened,
   delighting with their promise
   before their too short loveliness dissolved .
Some buds opened to unfold their glory,
   yet they, too, now have gone . . .

And we are left . . .
    to mourn their loss . . .
    and ask the endless questions
    to gather up the dreams and memories
      and fashion from the depth of our despair
A living, new bouquet . . .

Refined from the sadness at our center,
Risen from hard knowledge, newly gained,
Recreated from this love
    which is both our sorrow and our joy.

So that we may continue to bud,
    and to grow,
    and to bloom . . .
To share with others
    in ways before
      undreamed of
    Into a deeper,
more glowing,
    beauty!

A Walk in the Garden

Shoes off, at the dining room table,
I begin these words.
Outside, a weak sun casts soft shadows,
The Bay stirs in small waves.

I have just returned
    from walking in the garden . . .
Smells of spring greeted me.
The earth was fragrant with spring!

How strange, to discover this,
when my thoughts are connected
To earth, as a burial place.
The ambiguity of it all . . .
    it all!

In the garden, last year's plants lie dark,
Tangled stems and flower heads
awaiting the pruner's handiwork.
Green sprouts mingle in their midst.

Some bulbs were planted years ago.
Some last fall, with hope of this year's spring.
Oh hope and trust,
    now so sorely shaken!

Snowdrops and crocuses
    bloom in sunny places,
Seemingly so small, so fragile,
yet with a strength to rise
through last year's leaves.

I need that strength,
Flowing from deep roots within,
A place where there is bedrock
That even such a loss as mine
    can be cradled in.

I walk the stepping stones
Around the garden's edge,
Absorbed in spring discovery.
Are the new bulbs surfacing?

How can my heart absorb this beauty
At this time of wounds so deep and raw?
Yet I need so much this beauty!
Open . . . heart, and let this beauty in!

Open
    heart . . .
        and
           let this beauty
              in!

This Child of Mine

In the early days, after
   the death of this child of mine,
   there is only numbness
     and incomprehension . . .
that the sun continues to rise each morning
that my friends, loved ones, still smile
     and laugh.

My whole world has fallen away.
   Heart contracted to a mere mechanism,
   alternately shrivelled hard,
   or pounding alarmingly.
What kind of mother am I,
   whose child has died?

I search for reasons, "why?" . . . "why?"
I search for meaning in this terrible loss,
I search and search . . .
   for a reconciliation with self,
   for a forgiveness of self,
     for this mother whose child has died.

So slowly seeps new understanding . . .
So slowly pain permits its dissolution . . .
Yet over hard-walked time
   comes dispensation . . .
which calls forth changes from
   the depths of being.

A mother, now, who cradles other hearts
    whose songs are silent;
A mother who with love and outstretched arms
    accepts the gifts
    this child of mine has given . . .
An overwhelming, joyous offering
    of life with life
Now born anew a mother's love
    toward a broken world.

I Could Never Forget You!

In these first days and weeks
   through the haze
      I cannot believe . . .
      your death.

In the no-longer dream of
   your being amongst us,
In the no-longer sound of
   your shouts as you enter the door,
In the no-longer ring, and ring again,
   of the telephone by your friends,
In the no-longer lying awake listening
   for your coming home with the car,
In the no-longer cards, phone calls,
   and visits
   of your adult years . . .

No longer . . .
The anticipation of your birth
the wonder of your baby growth
the delight of your love of life
the worry of your mistakes
the future dreams and plans
   of your adulthood
   of our grandparenting,

No longer . . .

Yet I think of you constantly
and the pain of my loss
   overwhelms me.

Will there ever be a time
    when memories hold the love,
    without the hurt?
    hold hope of new meaning
    rather than despair?

Be still, my soul.
That I may dream and hope again . . .
That the power of your
    once presence with us
May dwell in a new way within my being
    that brings deeper meaning
    and new life within my heart.

I could never forget you!

All the Mothers

This is the month of Mother's Day,
A day so hard to live through
When thoughts concern a child now dead.
What formerly was celebration, now despair.

I think of all the saddened Mothers . . .
The cards, the advertisements for this Day,
That everywhere assail the eyes
Yet know estrangement from all joy.

I think of ones with now no living children,
and wonder what the feelings
of such a one would be.
No living child . . . and yet a mother always!

Where do all the feelings and the love flow?
The memories of the one so loved,
The love . . . where does it now
    find a place to live?
And find a place it must, o'er time.

I think of mothers with that empty place,
Around the table, in that aching heart.
Of siblings, with lives so different now,
Of families, torn from familiar moorings, adrift.

And I have known and I have heard
the words of mothers who have said,
that their lives became anew through mothering;
Grateful for the unknown depths
    that grew and blossomed.

How much too short, too short!
Yet what that life has meant
Remains now in my heart,
and needs to be rediscovered
    through this grief.

Our child, our children,
cradled in our mothering thoughts;
Nurtured by memory into our deepest being,
And living on in us as actions.

    That make a difference by our mothering,
    In this time and place in which now we live.
    Our children . . . ourselves . . . mothers still . . .
        To a new world waiting to be born!

A Mother's Thoughts

This is the time of year that tears
   at a mother's heart.
and in the early months and years of loss,
Mother's Day is fraught with
   'might have beens.'

For some, who only dreamt of mothering,
   there is the void, yet so much feeling.
Intimations and expectations gone awry,
Yet still the secret knowledge of 'your' being.

For many, memories are fused with sadness.
Your 'not being with us' is all we live with now.
We wonder at our mothering, now gone astray,
Sometimes wandering on a path of guilt.
Or on a path of anger, with self, others,
   or with God.
Maybe we stay depressed.
The meaning of our lives is rent apart,
   a gaping hole exists.
Are these the mother's thoughts YOU think?

Some slowly find a way to bring up
   memories that are sweet.
Your presence in our lives reverberates
   and comes to dance within our hearts
     at special times.

Our hearts dance too again, and offer thanks,
For this touching of our lives by you . . .
The thoughts of you;
      the good times and the bad;
How much we learned together,
      of family and love!

Is this the Mother's Day when you will find,
      deep in the heart of things, that suddenly,
the memories are now more glad than sad?

It does happen, many mothers say,
      along this path we walk,
Our child, our children, resting in our hearts,
The gladness and thanksgiving . . .
      the sadness and thanksgiving,
With all the varied feelings of our humanness.

How could we ever have imagined,
this journey we are called upon to make . . .
How a richness and a mellowness
      evolves at last,
From what has been discovered on the way.

Mother's Memories

There are so many memories . . .
The early fantasies of motherhood . . .
The dreamings of possibilities . . .
and then the expectancy . . .
   of YOU.
The long months of waiting . . .
   Your birth!
The inner questionings of new motherhood.
How you captured all my heart and life!

The moments, the days, the months,
   the years of you;
It differs for each mourning mother.
But to live without you
Has for each of us
So much in common.

We never dreamt that we would visit
At the graveside of our child.
We never could have known the void,
   created by your absence.
We never knew the bands of hurt
   in chest and throat and gut,
We never knew the tears that flowed,
   or would not flow,
The restless days,
The great dark fog of mind or
ceaseless churning in the head.
   But now we know.

We never understood before
The healing that may come to be
In the presence of a listening
     friend who silently accepts
     our words of grief.
When eyes meet in sorrow deep,
When arms embrace in care and love.

For we must speak so many times
Of our children who have died.
Who will listen as the months go by?
So often it is other mothers,
     bereft themselves,
Who offer and who find the healing
In the listening and the sharing.

Slowly, oh so slowly,
We relinquish that loved presence
Slowly, oh so slowly,
We bring up all the memories
     and place them tenderly within our heart.
     and place them lovingly within our heart.

And then as time goes by and we
     continue bringing out our
     memories into our opened heart
We find along this tortuous way
A place more calm and peaceful.

At last our memories
   are more of joy than pain,
As we integrate that loved life
   within our own,
And it seems now that the living
   and the dying of our child,
Brings a new compassion
   to our lives.
Our child's life lives on,
   within our new formed life,
In that strange mystery of soul
That unites us all
In the great Creator's Arms.

Thinking of Fathers
on Father's Day
...By a Mother...

It hurts, these days, to remember back,
to days of innocence and youth;
to days of meeting, and of early love,
with every hour a newness to unfold.

Then promises were made
and dreams came true;
and in all the world
there was only you!

And then a seed was planted and enclosed
within a womb, to grow;
Love uniting to bring life anew
and joy was sweet with expectation.

And then a child was born;
the wonder of it all!
This greatest of all gifts
for us to nourish and protect.

For some, the hours and days were few,
for some, the years flew by.
For all ... whose child has died,
the wound is deep inside.

How did this great loss come to be?
and why, for my loved child?
And what was there I could have done?
So many questions; so few answers.

It seems I cannot comprehend
the untimeliness of it all.
To be the parent of a child who died
feels like a robber tearing out the heart.

And I must weep for my great loss;
for the loss of my child to the world;
for the times that might have been;
for the family, and families,
that might have been.

And then, along the path of grief
a question comes to mind,
and asks me gently what my child
would want for me . . . now.

Slowly, oh so slowly, I ponder the response;
Slowly, oh so slowly . . . father and mother,
sometimes separately, sometimes together,
the days and months and years go by.

How difficult to speak and share
    this hurt and pain
where formerly the words and lives entwined.
To live through times of anger,
    guilt and sadness,
to finally release the feelings that are
    there . . . into Creation's bosom.

To find the peace that passeth understanding
as the tears and the tensions flow
into that greater love surrounding all;
that holds each breaking heart
   with tender passion.

And gently through that special love,
sometimes human, sometimes divine,
I'll find a way to recreate
a new wholeness from the brokenness.

For my child's life will keep on
living in my heart,
and reshape my life, and all relationships
in deeper, loving, harmony.

How can it be?!!
It is so unbearably, unutterably painful
to learn so much of life's great lessons
from the dying of my child!

And so, dear one, the father of our child,
Let us grieve together when we can,
   separately when we must;
That the love of our child,
   the love for our child,
may live on, within us, and between us.

Loss of a Love

I had never known . . .
   the swift, deep cut of intense pain
   that surges through the chest and throat
   that grabs the guts with vise-like hold.

I had never known . . .
   the long, grey days of isolation
   of 'no more joy'
   of 'so little hope.'

I had never known . . .
   the paralysis of living,
   the clock that ticks and ticks
   in time with nothingness.

I could not comprehend . . .
   that the sun still comes up each day,
   that spring would loosen still the buds
   held tight in winter's sway.

I could not comprehend . . .
   how others went their normal way,
   (and it might seem that I did too)
   in the knowledge of my desolation.

I could not comprehend . . .
   that others expected me, so soon,
   to get along with my life;
   time enough had passed, they said.

Slowly, oh so slowly . . .
    could I lift my eyes again
    and see anything but sadness and despair,
and feel anything but constriction
    and unbalance.

Slowly, oh so slowly . . .
    did the numbness, anger, guilt,
    the resentment and unfairness of it all
    begin to release my heart from hell.

Slowly, oh so slowly . . .
    could I deal with all the changes
    in my outward life,
    in my inner being.

There was still a need . . .
    to acknowledge and to live
    with painful feelings,
    to acknowledge sometimes guilt and anger.

There was still a need . . .
    to change, never again
    would I be the same.
    The fear of discovering a new me!

And now, along my journey . . .
    I hold new knowingness
    it permeates my being,
    it plants my feet on firm ground.

And now, along my journey . . .
　　there are scars, but mostly healed,
　　there are new friendships,
　　deeper, and more satisfying.

And now, along my journey . . .
　　One can reach out,
　　as a wounded healer,
　　to some whose feet tread newly on this path.

For now I know . . .
　　a new found meaning for such words
　　as pain, and friend, and love.
　　(the agony of one's child as a teacher).

For now I know . . .
　　that somehow he still lives;
　　the spirit that inhabits all of life
　　is deep within the soul of each of us.

This Hard Time
and Space

I saw the face of pain today,
Myself, in a mirror, newly bereaved.
Struggling for some form of self-control
When life feels absolutely uncontrollable.

The words of death and loss
So difficult to say at first,
The feelings of such desolation
so cold and empty, so alone.

The days and weeks go by . . .
How can they, when my child is dead?
Stop the world! Can't you see?
That my child is dead!!

Can I even partially respond
To that outstretched hand,
Those eyes that see, into my heart, so hurt?
Will I reach out, to such understanding?

There is so much confusion,
Feelings I have never known before.
They make me wonder if I'm going crazy.
They make me wonder if I will survive.

Must I stay within this isolation
To protect the sanity I have?
What would happen if I dared to share
With others who have walked this path before?

And then I wonder at that old, old story,
of the One who sent a Son,
of that Son who walked His path
and that Father who became bereaved.

The story says He loves us so,
and calls us to a Resurrection;
to re-birth after such a death;
I scarce can even ponder this.

Yet, I have heard the words of newness,
and know the acts of kindness
that only such a newness does explain,
from others who have walked ahead.

So now it is my turn
to gather up the memories and the love,
and place them, oh so gently,
    in my heart,
So gently,
        in
            my heart.

Summer

Tranquility

The pond lay tranquil
in the early morning light.
Surface smooth as glass
reflecting, in symmetry,
   a place beyond.

Since that one day
there is no tranquility.
Waves threaten to overwhelm.
The depths are stirred and changed.
Will this storm subside?

Slowly, so very slowly,
the wildness recedes.
Within and around the pond
nothing is the same.

Churned out of the depths
from places known not before.
What once lay hidden
   now lies exposed,
      seeking new comprehension.

No more the harmony once known.
Where is the beauty in
   this new creation
      thrust savagely
         upon this well-loved place?

Through pain and loneliness
Through friends who love and care
   comes an integration
     born of old and new
     spangles of light refract
       diamonds on the pond's surface.

The pond dreams tranquil once again.
    New treasures of the heart
Give quiet thanks.
   Give loving thanks.

The Way . . . of Grief

At first I stayed
   in my cocoon,
   in a fog
   of protective greyness.

Then, on my way of grief
   one day . . .
   The cocoon opened
   and I was walking
     along a rocky path
     in the sharp pain
     in the dark night
   with my thoughts of sorrow.

At first I thought I was alone
   so alone, upon this road.
Yet, sometimes, when a star shone
I saw another . . . and another . . .
walking this same hard way.

We stumbled along together,
   at times . . .
It became less lonely,
   at times . . .
As I walked with the pain of my grief.

Much later, now . . .
   along the way,
the sharp stones worn smoother now
   from walking, walking, walking . . .
The darkness turned to dawning. Grief no
longer stabs incessantly;
Pain now blunted from my walk with grief;
Friends are by my side
   who have walked with me!

A new day comes at last
   after all this time.
The memories . . .
   now soft and warm
   with just an
   occasional sharp stab
    of pain and longing.

I am forever changed
   by you who were
    my flesh.
Your life within mine,
As I walk along
   my way.

The loved ones,
   woven into my heart and life
    in a new way
That brings acceptance
that brings peace and thanks . . . giving!

Patterns

Great blue heron stands motionless
   at the end of the rocks each sunrise;
Patterns of sun and shade
   on the late summer grass
      change imperceptibly with the suns' arc;
Tides ebb and flow in pattern
   with the moon's slow path;
Friends speak of their usual small annoyances,
   and larger victories;
Relatives discuss, with that same mixture
   of familiarity and
      maliciousness, the latest family faux pas;
and the
   sun
      continues
         to rise
         each
            morning . . .
How can this be?
   In that moment when our child died
   Or that miscarriage
     or that stillbirth occurred,
in
   that
     one
       moment
    All is changed
       and
Will never be that same again.

How can the world go on its patterned path?
How can our friends continue
   in their trivial pursuits?
How can the school year
   begin without our child?
How can the sun and the moon
   still pattern the day and the night?
      No patterns continue to sustain us,
      We tremble at the void's edge,
But wait!
Outstretched arms enfold
Understanding shines deeply
   from eyes that know
Days and months and years go by
Pain and anger and guilt and sorrow are borne
To become a new day . . .
Patterned of suffering and of love
   of understanding and of acceptance.
And the greatest of these . . . is LOVE.

Garden of Remembrance

In this summer-lateness dusk
The Garden dreams a peace.
My heart, so often full of knots,
Relaxes, feels at ease.

Walking round the hourglass path,
Towards the sundial at far end,
The grass is as a carpet green
Providing a magic flying tour.

First the Garden of Louisa Catherine,
Wife of John Quincy Adams,
Family roots a few miles thither.
Memories of early history stir.

Then comes a weathered sundial,
Centered in a Fragrance Garden.
Lavender and herbs so sweetly mingle,
I'm overwhelmed with so much loveliness.

I see the outlined shape of pedestal and sundial,
Think of grieving parents who gave this gift,
And hope their hearts are deeply calmed,
By this timeless, fragrant beauty.

Turning and continuing along the path,
A luxuriant garden comes in view;
First the bounty of a butterfly bush,
Newly opening tiny purple
    blooms on long racemes.
All other plants chosen purposefully
To provide the nectar food required
To cajole butterflies to flutter by,
To stay awhile, in this special garden.

Beside this garden, next to
    heliotrope and bee balm,
A bench of cedar invites a tarrying time.
This bench was given by
    The Compassionate Friends,
In memory and in honor of our children.

So, bide a'wee . . .
It fills one's heart to be in such a place,
A kaleidoscope of thoughts and feelings,
Of the ones we keep now in memory,
Of the ones who fill our hearts with love.

Let this become a sacred place,
Where memory and love can mingle,
Midst this place of peace and beauty,
As the butterflies flit by . . .

Now, moving on, along the path,
A wilder prairie garden is in sight.
A Garden to remember Margaret Mackall Smith,
    born here near this garden,
Married later to President Zachary Taylor.

The wind blows, in the flowers and the grasses,
Bending them, moving them, changing them.
We who know the death of children,
Also know of bending, moving, changing.

It is somehow heart enlarging,
To be here, so separate yet together.
Honoring, remembering, loving,
     hurting, healing . . . and also uplifted,
By this place of peace and beauty,
By this time here in the garden.

Reflections

I have cried the tears of
    a sadness and a madness
    never even dreamed of . . .

I have clenched my hands and heart,
    and carried on in
        never to be acknowledged despair . . .

I have known an isolation
    that separates me from
    all human connectedness . . .

I have forced myself,
    with heart like stone,
        to do the things that must be done,
            at this dreadful time.

I have received from friends and strangers,
    an outpouring of great love,
        that reaches deep within . . .

I have found that many cannot help.
    I don't yet have the strength to be
    the understanding one . . .

I have felt the fear of being the parent
    whose child has died.
So much feels like failure . . .

I have known the utter inability,
    to be available to my other children.
    Sometimes even to acknowledge
        their new needs . . .

I have asked how can the sun still rise,
  and others go about their tasks.
It all seems so incomprehensible to me . . .

I have asked the questions of life's meaning,
And of a God they say is caring
And waited for the touch of loving arms . . .

I have sat in silent hope and meditation,
To receive the solace of that One,
Known by intuition and deep reverie . . .

I have known the days and
  months and years go by,
And found the hurt less painful
And found the memories now bittersweet . . .

I now accept these new deep learnings,
As the gift my child has given;
Our lives now interwoven
  in memory and action . . .

And once again life calls for living,
In ways undreamed of formerly . . .
In ways more deep and loving . . .

A Long, Slow Journey

In these slow hot days of summer,
When air is scarcely breathing
And a greyed world surrounds
My listlessness

Only the wild beating of a heart,
The raging thoughts within a mind,
The tight agony of a throat in tears,
Speak of living.

This living is like none known before.
More like a living death
Are these first weeks and months.
My child, my child, now gone.

Sometimes there comes a short reprieve.
I see a lily's speckled petals.
I hear the wings of hummingbirds.
Someone looks me in the eye

And softly asks, "How are you?"
And I receive a message
That I can truthfully respond!
And gratitude and love are mingled.

This journey through the valley
Is difficult, and different
For each of us.
Let gentleness pour down!

Let us not ask too much
Of ourselves . . .
This is a wounded time.
Let us care about our healing.

And do the things that
Inwardly feel liberating.
Slowly, slowly, let our steps
Find the haven that's renewing.

So now our child lives on
Within our memory . . .
Enriched by that child so loved
And our own long hard journey.

Seeing once again the beauty,
Reaching out to others hurting,
Gathering all the riches known
Into a Thanksgiving tapestry . . .

Dying . . . and Living

It came . . .
like a message from hell;
 the words, "Your child is dead."
The utterly inexplicable, unacceptable,
 information.
The immediate response, "This cannot be!".

Those words . . .
cut at the heart of
 an up-till-now gloriously pregnant woman,
they cut at the hearts of
 mothers, fathers, siblings, grandparents . . .
 for a stillborn lying quiet and shining . . .
 a newborn, whose great struggle was
  unable to succeed . . .
 a baby, overwhelmed suddenly by SIDS . . .
 the children, in their young years, in
  accidents so diverse, yet results so
  sadly similar . . .
 the young ones, with genetic handicaps, or
  birth traumas, fighting on and on;
  yet finally, a death . . .
 the teenagers, overcome by events out of
  their control; or suddenly,
  out of control in their own lives;
  their invincibility a shattered body . . .
 those ones who saw no hope, who chose in
  sudden action, or through long
  pondered desperation . . . suicide . . .

those ones for whom rage and hate and
   violence shattered lives . . .
those ones who died on foreign soil, or in
   foreign skies or seas, for this land
   whose dream they dreamed . . .
and lately come the ones who died of AIDS,
   unknowing this new curse upon our earth
   and then the older ones, our children
   still, whose lives are shortened
   by disease or accident . . .

We gather them all up . . . each one unique!
We bring them to our wounded hearts,
And hold them with a fierceness and a love,
And ask how we can go on living,
Yet knowing that we must.
And ask sometime along the road of grief
How we can turn a dying to a living?

They have gone before . . .
It is so hard to reconcile . . .
And we are left . . .
   to draw together all these strands
   of our own lives we've lived till now,
   and weave into the threads not broken
   a pattern up till now unguessed at.

We must bring into our tapestry
    the threads that glisten with our
        children's lives,
    and add our own new threads of deeper
        understanding, and of
        profound reverence for life,
    and weave these hard-found strands
    to make a pattern more inclusive,
        and with greater depth;
    a mosaic that brings
        new beauty and compassion
    that forms deeper human friendships
        and communities.

All these things . . .
    and more . . .
    can come to be
because of my child,
    my children.
And sometime . . .
    a long way down
    this unknown road,
I will give thanks . . .
    in a new way . . .
        once again.

Time, Untimeliness, Timelessness

To wake in the pale stillness of a summer dawn,
The Bay mirror calm, haze in the east;
Then suddenly, the red blaze of a hot sun
    coming from behind a low-banked cloud.

A narrow, blood-red streak
parts the still grey waters.
It cuts into my heart like a knife . . .
separating the before, the after, of my days.

Three great blue herons fly across the water.
I see the heavy flapping of their wings
in tune and time with age-old wisdom
that rises so effortlessly, from within.

I wish it could be so for me;
Where is the wisdom that I seek?
For now, my mind darts like a dragonfly,
Or else, lies muffled in its head cocoon.

My world has changed.
There is great sadness, and despair
    not known before.
My time has been slashed by the
untimeliness of my child's death.

In the first days and weeks,
I am consumed by the loss.
The 'no longer with me' of that one,
Born of love and longing for new birth.

And then there are the anniversaries,
    of birthdays, holidays, death days,
That loom with pain and dread;
"How can I ever get through the day?"

The sun is higher now;
Crab boats move as silhouettes on silver water.
It is summer once again;
The days drone on.

Suddenly, by the hummingbird feeder,
    a flash awakens my listlessness.
Fast fluttering wings, long beak
    feeding drip by drip,
Then plunging deep into the sweetness
    of red flowers.

Time moves on.
For us, whose child has died,
There is a timeliness for mourning,
There is a timeliness for living.

Not the automation of the feathered ones,
Rather, the slow . . . deep . . . needed . . .
   acceptance
  and outpouring of the heart's emotions
And the mindful doing of our now
   changed lives.

Time moves on . . .
The grief less painful and continuous now.
Yet this one event has altered
How I think, and see, and do.

I've walked a path not chosen,
Know a way more deep; alone, yet not alone . . .
For somehow, now, the very essence
  of my child
Lives on in ways undreamed of.

And now I seek both depths and heights,
Enlarging spaces where my soul can soar;
A wider, more inclusive, seeking love,
That binds together . . . lifts . . .
   ennobles all of life!

Summer Picnic

The flowers bloom their beauty,
The breeze, still cool, this early hour,
Birds singing their morning song,
The sun rises from Bay waters,
To place its golden presence there.
Ah! The beauty of it all!
Ah! the aching of that beauty
Upon my frozen heart.

It is the day of the picnic.
And I will bake the beans,
And do the other things I must.
Yet much of me is in a fog,
Wondering how can this ever be?
I want to scream, "Not me! Not me!"
Preparing to attend a picnic
With families whose children have died.

Yet I will go, for I have gone before,
And know the love and kindness there,
Of those others
Who have walked this path,
And know that being
With those others,
Is a part of my own healing.
And know that, the receiving
And giving of deep understanding
Makes the road less lonely,
Makes me feel
More human once again.

And we will speak of ordinary things,
And . . . extraordinary . . . things,
But always with deep attention.
And a deep compassion flows . . .

If I allow that tight cocoon to open,
To receive those messages of love,
If I allow that other in my life,
To share our common hurt and need.

And I know, before we go our separate ways,
That the love with each breaking heart
Will somehow have been validated.
Even in the absence of our child.
The balloons carrying each name
   Of all those listed monthly in
      "Our Children Remembered"
Will have been released, and watched,
And pondered . . . in our hearts.

And those of us who baked the beans,
And did other ordinary things,
    For a summer picnic
    Will know a sadness and a tenderness
That somehow leads to healing.
    And for those of you not present,
    We held you in our hearts . . .
    Your children . . .
        And our children . . .
            Together.
Never to be forgotten!

Summer Thoughts

I wake these summer mornings
    in a sloth of discontent . . .
Nothing seems the way it used to be.
What shall I do with my life,
    now that my child has died?
It takes so very long,
    to accept the unacceptable.
Over and over in my mind,
The endless questions,
    the endless *if only's*
    and the *why's*
"How can this possibly be?"

I feel so alone, so very isolated
    from all other beings.
Has anyone ever felt the feelings,
    and thought the thoughts that I now know?
Can I ever have the trust and courage to share
    these overwhelming feelings?
Will they say that I am crazy,
    for I sometimes wonder if I am.

I have never felt this way before.
    What shall I do?
    What SHALL I do?

We must each decide the way
   we walk this journey.
It is a rocky road that leads
   into the valley, or scales
   the mountain where new
   vistas open out.
It is mine to choose.
   I place one foot ahead,
   then often slip behind.
But I must choose for life,
My child would want it so.

I struggle so, yet must go on.

I look to find the ways that help.

Others have walked this road before me,
   and they have great compassion.
They know so much that I now know,
   yet rant at knowing.
Somehow, in their presence,
   it is less lonely;
Somehow, in their presence,
   I see they are surviving;
Somehow, in their presence,
   I find trust again;

Somehow, in their presence,
　　Hope visits in my heart,
And I dare to believe that once again,
Life will be beautiful,
And for a moment, there is peace!

My spirit needed that respite so much . . .
I am thankful from a place
　　deep within my heart . . .

Slowly, oh so slowly,
I can allow the memories of my
　　beloved child to surface,
And there now is joy
　　amidst the pain.
And I am grateful for that life
　　and for the memories,
And for the living power
　　of those memories
　　　in my life!

Death . . .

Yet Life Goes On . . .

Summer is here.
Out in the fields of July . . .
   the early morning mist arises
Out on the Bay and the creeks
   the sun rises red though haze.

The days go by,
   I scarcely notice,
In the first days
   of this terrible loss
It seems incredible that the sun
Still follows its course.
My life and my world have been
   so indelibly changed.

I want to scream and scream,
   to rage and howl,
Other times, to just curl up
   forever in a dark room.
Is it possible to survive?
Do I want to survive?

My son . . . my daughter . . .
So much a part of my life.
To let go of your presence,
Of future hopes and dreams . . .
My heart feels severed.
You were so much a part of my heart.

Slowly, slowly,
The letting go takes place.
As the mist and haze of summer
Obscure the fields and waters,
Yet the fields and waters remain . . .
So, finally,
New understanding dawns . . .

You are here now . . .
In a new way . . .
In the memories that fill
 my heart with thanksgiving,
In the mist and haze that
 veil the totality of it all,
In the presence of your spirit
 with my own,
In the unending seamlessness
 of that ALL !!!

The Storm

The rain stormed across the Bay,
Rivulets ran down the new dug soil,
Petals of blossoms blew in the wind,
The storm raced on.

My storm is in the heart.
It pounds suddenly,
Pulling tight bands across my chest;
It heaves and sighs,
It moans and cries.

My storm is in the mind,
Its memory loss, confusing thoughts;
A mind now full of fuzzy grey
Or suddenly, racing and overwrought.

My storm is in the eyes,
Staring into the distances for a child so loved;
A silhouette that catches in a crowd,
Eyes that stay wide open in the night
When sleep is longed for;
Eyes that silently release the tears,
Or a sobbing, heaving mix of great despair.

My storm is in the emotions.
The swiftness of an anger never known before,
The stab of guilt . . . "if only . . ."
Depression that deepens
    to a bottom dark and lonely.
The ups and downs as on a stormy sea.

All this . . . and more,
That seems to be the way of grief,
That fills a parent's days
   whose child has died.

And yet . . .
A time does come,
When some new joy or beauty
Catches at a grieving heart
And slowly lightens up the greyness . . .

The opening of a flower,
The song a wild bird sings,
The sun at daybreak on the Bay's horizon,
The kindness of a friend,
The thought that comes unbidden
   of memories of our child,
The hope that enters
   that deep, lonely place
   when love is present,
The thankfulness
   that that one life existed . . .
   though far too short . . .
So overwhelming
   in its impact
      on my heart!

A Grief Path

It is summer.
The sun rises orange upon the Bay
Its path on the water one great golden swath.
There is no answering flame within my heart.

The woodpecker knocks upon the dead tree.
The vibrations pass by my ear, unreceived.
Nothing can enter my consciousness,
    Walled off alone by my sorrow.

Please support me, my friends
In this devastating time.
I dimly know how hard this is for you
A stranger to the ways of grief.

One phones me, ready always to listen
To my long story, or my few slow words.
I love her for her constancy.
I need, so much, the warmth of love.

One, who knows, says it will get better.
My heart, wanting to believe
Files away a sliver of hope.
I need, so much, rekindled hope.

Day by day, week after week,
    month after month,
It may be year after year,
My heart reopens slowly
    to love grown deeper,
My spirit reborn with wiser hope!

Summer's Soundings

The pace of summer days is slow.
The heat of early morning orange sun
Shimmers on the waters of the Bay,
On silhouettes of gulls against the glare,
The sudden raucous gru-uck of a close-by heron.

The heat, the shadows deep, soft sounds of water,
Allow for a certain somnolence . . .
Mind turns slowly in this summer haze
To days gone by . . . to a family whole . . .

Hesitantly, pulling at the closet of my mind,
Setting, suddenly, the door wide open,
What tumbles out, from places dark and deep,
To be discarded, or examined yet anew.

Remembrance of that child, so precious,
The miracle of bonds of parenthood,
Everyday becomes a first time newness.
To see a young mind wakening to creation,
Challenging a parent on to further growth.

And then a death . . . how could it be?
HOW COULD IT BE???
The disbelief, the rage,
    the overwhelming load of dark despair.
In self-protection, shut the door on feelings!

Life goes on, e'en that of parents so bereaved.
So much stacked into the closet . . . closed.
What is outside becomes truncated.
Yet each heart decides how this will be.

To take out all the memories, one by one,
To own and feel the feelings they engender,
To feel them in our heart and gut so deeply,
To ponder the significance . . . it sets us free!

Free to remember good and bad,
Free to speak and laugh and rage and love,
Free to bring the memory of that beloved child
Into the light, into each day's encounter.

Free to use the learnings from our child
With others who walk newly on this way,
Free to have no secrets, shame and guilt
For it is time to discard useless things.

We will work well the creation of this day.
This day we live . . . to-day.
Now so enriched and freed,
With the wholeness that is now ours to claim.

We thank you, our children of love and life.
I thank you John Michael Andrews.

Flying High

The geese flew over today
    great honking cries up high
    the wavering arc etched on and on
    against the blue of the sky

I wondered at their constancy,
    their many seasons' flights
    and how they know intuitively
    as with an inner sight

I long for inner sight myself
    to light the darkened days
    since my child's light extinguished
    on that sad remembered day.

How amidst confusion
    will head stay above the storm
    my travels in this different world
    leave life without its form.

Now as the geese move on each day
    their destiny ahead
    I'll take each moment one by one
    and go the way my heart is led.

Trusting that when love awakens
    e'en amidst this sadness now
    a day will come when spirit lightens
    So let my soul now know this power!

I Never Knew . . .

I never knew . . .
   so much despair
   such depths of anguish
   such wild emotions

I never knew . . .
   such long grey days
   such nights of questioning
   such unendurable
             loneliness

I never knew . . .
   the fear some others have
   about my loss
   the kindness of some people
   and how difficult
      it sometimes is
      to accept.

I never knew . . .
   such learning within my mind
   such strength within my heart
   such depths within my soul.

And now I know
   receiving and giving
   sorrow and deep joy
   thankfulness and love

My child, my son.
How could I have learned
   so much from you?

I never knew . . .
   the dull expanse of days
   the wild beating of a broken heart.

I never knew . . .
   the wetness of continuous tears
   the dryness of unspoken sobs.

I never knew . . .
   the body's strange reaction
      to emotional pain
   the mind's overwhelming grief
      when one's child has died.

I never knew . . .
   that there are those
   who through their own
      wounded hearts
   now know the ways
      that speak with tenderness and love
      to those with fresh-felt grief.

I never knew . . .
   how much I would need
      to drop my pride and independence
   and so allow another's tenderness
      to slip into my life.

I never knew . . .
　　that even as an island,
　　　seemingly alone,
　　I also am amongst all other islands
　　in an ocean cradled lovingly
　　in the ceaseless caring of creation.

I never knew . . .
　　the difference that a single
　　　act of kindness makes
　　upon a heart bereft;
　　and now with heartfelt wonder
　　and great thanksgiving
　　sing a new song
　　　to all who care!

Now, in my memory
　　my child lives on.
　　That living and that dying
　　　of one so loved by me,
　　now creates in me
　　　a new born self . . .
　　Melded in the fire of grief
　　Moulded of the joy and the sorrow
　　　that IS LIFE!!

Fall

A New Season

In this new season of the year . . .
   the leaves wither and fall.
   The beauty of each leaf,
   the beauty of each tree,
     that formerly entranced me
     is now scarcely seen.

My eye seems to model my sadness,
   selectively seeing the
     dying of gardens and greenery;
   blind to the beauty of it all . . .
     in this first fall
       after the death
         of my child.

The memories overwhelm . . .
   small feet trampling on brown leaves
   the wonderful crunchy sound of it all,
   the laughter, the joy, of it all,
     I miss it so.
   the hikes to the mountains
     covered in reds and gold;
   the tidelands brown turning
     beside the blue waters;
   It all seems so dull, without meaning.

Yet, I cannot allow this for the
    rest of my life.
    I must find a way to move forward.
My child would be sad, disappointed,
    at my self-absorption
It hurts to admit that my child
    would be repulsed
    by my now self . . .

What is it I must do to move forward?

I must acknowledge that I do have choices.

    I can choose to take a small step
        into the future,
        or not to take that step;

I can choose to respond negatively or
    positively to another's overtures
    of friendship;
I can choose to accept support that may help,
    or not to accept that support;
I can choose to see the colors of fall . . .
    whether to dwell on beauty,
    or unceasingly, on death;
    whether to get up and do . . . something,
    or remain passive and lethargic.

These small choices
    can eventually
        make great differences.
They slowly form the outlines
    of my life ahead . . .

Whether it will have a meaning
    that encompasses my child's life
    and all that has been known . . .
    that includes the sorrow and the joy
    that moves on
        with all those learnings . . .
    to evolve along a path now
        broadened and deepened
        yet strangely shining in a new way . . .
            because of my child.

Let me gather the fragrance and
    beauty of each hour
and move up the mountain in this
    golden season.

September Thoughts

As the daylight shortens
As the heat lessens
As the flowers of summer
Give way to chrysanthemums and
    the leaves of gold . . .
I ponder . . .

The no-moreness of Fall activities
    with my child . . .
No more . . . the dreams of pushing
    the stroller in the coolness,
No more . . . the first days of day care,
    of pre-school, of school
No more . . . the ritual preparation
    of back to school
Though my eyes see all the
    usual signs in the Mall,
    amongst the neighbors.
My heart lies so heavy at this
    no-moreness of my days.

Even midst the needs of siblings
That no-moreness of the missing one
Screams silently . . . or not so silently,
"Why are you here no more? How can this be?"

For those whose child was older,
Away from home perhaps
The no-moreness finds itself
In the absence of phone calls, the visits,
New relationships with grandchildren,
    with in-laws,
Sometimes overwhelming,
Sometimes now so difficult to sustain.

And there are others
Those with no surviving children
Now wondering what to do with parenting,
With a loss so great,
Sometimes it is a single parent,
Who must now, somehow, refill
    that terrible hole
Torn from a life once whole.

A heart and gut so raw and hurting
Needs so much tender care
From the owner of that body
And from so many others
To show that love is there, and cares.

As the days and weeks and months go by
How to live each moment? . . .
Striving for a new rebalancing
Caring for the body, mind and soul
Looking deeply inward to discover . . .
Those things that create new meaning,
Those things that lead to trust and peace.

For most, this way is long,
Yet also a journey extraordinary
For on the way discoveries are made
That fill our being at levels
    formerly not known . . .
That dry well can become
    a fountain of sweet water?
Refreshing the wanderer
And o'erflowing even
To enliven others walking by.

The Ways of Love

A heart encircles with dreams
   the lives of those we love . . .
      dreams for that life as it unfolds;
      dreams for our life
         in relation to that life;
      hopes for that life,
         that there may be . . .
         the closeness of infancy,
         the delights of childhood,
         the growth of adolescence,
         the satisfactions of young adulthood,
         the lives of a new formed family,
            of grandchildren,
            and of our grandparenting.

Somewhere along the way,
      for us,
         these dreams have shattered.

We hold these fragments of our dreams
   in uncomprehending minds . . .
      we ask the *why's*
      we say the *if only's*
We feel the pain of loss and dreams,
      of suddenly ended lives
      cut short far too soon,
   and ponder how this came to pass,
   and ponder all the things that
      might have been.

A heart of love gropes for surcease of pain,
A heart of love longs for the one, now gone,
A heart of love . . . bereft . . .
      some time . . .
      some place . . .
Receives an unexpected act of love,
   and hope's flame lights a heart once more,
A heart of love can love once more!

O you, who now have healing hearts,
O you, for whom love's mem'ries shine with joy,
Reach out now,
   from understandings newly born
   and touch a heart of love
   whose flame burns low;
That from the love created by your child
   and from the heart of love within your heart,
There may be healing of another's heart!

'Those' Days, Holy - Days

The thoughts keep coming up.
   oft times we put them far aside;
Yet they return, over and over again,
"How will we ever get through that special day?"

It may be the first year for the Holidays,
It may be the second, or the third!
It may be the anniversary of a birthday . . .
How can we possibly survive such days?

It may be another kind of family day.
A day of special meaning now forever changed:
No longer the first day of the school year,
No longer a Halloween costume to complete;
Not again, will the feelings be the same,
for Veterans Day, or Memorial Day,
for Mother's Day, or Father's Day.
So much is changed.

It may be that first anniversary of the day
of your child's, your children's, death(s).
No! No! No! And yet we know that,
that day, too, comes 'round.

For some, the chosen way, is to be numb;
To remain in that grey fog that first envelopes us;
To not allow the enormity of the loss to penetrate.
This way, we never do our mourning;
We end up living in the past . . . alone
   with fantasies,
That allow no forward movement in our lives.

For others, not accustomed to such pain,
Without knowledge of the healing ways of grief;
Respond to culture's siren call, to 'get over it'.
They rush ahead, 'willing' all be well,
and cover up the feelings dwelling there within.

Some other ones, who can choose
    the mourning journey,
Begin along the painful path
That is the only route to deepest healing.

These holidays . . .
They give us a chance
To begin the journey through our grief;
We need to honor and respect our feelings,
For they represent our truest self.

How could we not have such emotions?
All our love and hopes and dreams
    seem shattered.
Let us now begin
To acknowledge all this pain,
Let us bring it from the depths within,
That we may tend it truly in the light of living,
And receive the balm of other wounded healers.

Let us now discover,
What our heart needs at this time.
Discover, also, needs of other grieving loved ones,
At this time of family mem'ries.

What plans can help to ease
The living of these days?

Let us think ahead, to know,
Where the holiday events must change,
Where we need a sameness,
To bring a calming peace to our
    frenetic thoughts.

Choose how remembrance can be done
(even through a breaking heart).
May a new kind of presence now begin,
(though changed forever, all is no longer lost).

As we allow new thoughts and feelings,
    on these special, sacred days.
There sometimes comes in fleeting moments
The faintest glimmer of a new Thanksgiving;
A warming presence that abideth once again
    in these Holy-days.

Holiday Reflections

My thoughts go back and forth,
    back and forth,
      wondering how this time could come
        to be . . .
My feelings go down and down,
    only very occasionally is there
    an upward beat . . .
My actions go from complete inaction,
    to spasmodic, compulsive doings,
    and back again, in withdrawal . . .
My soul feels mostly numb,
    unable to comprehend
    the spirit of the Season . . .
      in this first year of my loss.

My thoughts flit from
    the reality of this season,
    to the reality of this great absence . . .
Feelings of loss flood across
    the business of these days.
    They come in overwhelming waves
    upheaving the hard-won semblance
      of 'normality' . . .

My actions still fragmented,
   concentrated here . . . there . . . everywhere
      in a wild attempt
   to capture the ways of yesteryear . . .
My spirit is searching to know again
   the meaning of these holy days
   in the midst of confusion and chaos . . .
      in the early years of my loss.

My spirit now expanded,
   includes both joy and sorrow,
   yet rises on the breath of life
   to light a flame of hope
      and benediction.
I light the candle
   that its glow may soften
   every heart where deep despair
      holds sway.
I seek the star
   that guides
   a wounded heart along the way.
I know the hope
   that love can open wide
   the fast held tightness
      of deep loss

And Peace can find its place again
within a heart made
   newly whole once more.

Wholly, Holy!

Fruitfulness is everywhere;
    The great harvest moon shines
        warm and gold,
    Roadside stands o'erflow
        with season's harvest;
    Pumpkin piles along the roadside.
This bounty makes a mockery
    of my empty heart.
How many harvest moons before I know
    fullness and warmth and love again?
    Before my soul can trust again?
Yet many say these memories, through pain,
    can once more bring into my heart great joy;
That a deeper knowing, and a greater love,
    will once more bind my heart and soul again.
O Infinite One,
    I pray for that time.

Those Days

Those days.....
The special anniversaries,
The holidays,
They intrude into our thoughts
As nightmares,
After the death of our child.

Everything is now so changed,
Irrevocably.
Yet the holidays come up,
    seemingly unchanging
In our so-changed world.

There is such a disconnect
Between the way it was, and now is.
Halloween, Veterans' Day,
    Thanksgiving, Hanukkah,
    Christmas, the New Year
Shrouded now in grief, in unreality.
The music making mockery in my heart.

What shall I do with these holidays?
How does a broken heart contain
    the present pain
Yet include the reverence of the day?

Each must choose, decide,
The actions of the day . . .
Some let surviving children
    create new ways,
Some choose a day with no
    similarity to what was before,
Some search to find new rituals
    to give meaning to such loss.

Seeking ways to bring the one so loved,
Anew into a lonely heart,
Anew unto the new ones gathered . . .
Sharing memories and stories,
Planting a tree or garden,
Lighting a special candle on that day,
Giving a gift to someone else's need.
Creating special ways to kindle hearts
Into thanksgiving and remembrance.

All these things . . .
They speak of love . . .
A semblance of the love we yearn to hold.
It is not the same . . .
Yet it shows forth love,
It can be a beginning,
A new way for love to be a-borning
In this world, in this heart,
In remembrance and in honor of
Our love for our child . . .
A Thanksgiving for the life
And for the love of our child.

Surviving

Some days the pain seems unbearable
    and never ending.
I ask in despair,
What can I do
    to survive this time?

So I let this pain remain conscious,
and remember my child
    and the love I have known
And the gifts I have received
    from this one I have loved . . .

The good times and the not so good times
    that have been part of
    our loving and knowing each other
And in the midst of the pain
I give thanks for that loving and that knowing.

I would have wished to know much more . . .
Looking back now,
    after many years
On occasion there still come
    the quick sharp pangs of regret
    of never knowing
      some aspects
    of what will never be . . .

More often, there are
    the deeply satisfying understandings
    gained in the fire of despair
    and new actions now taken
    that may never have been
Without that searing pain.
Without the life of my child.

And I wonder . . . and give thanks . . .
    for what has been revealed to me
Because of this child of mine.

A Season of Change

The days go by
After the death of our child.
At first, in a daze of not-comprehension,
Wracked with wild outbursts, or tight control.

September is a month of change.
School begins, the early habitual preparations.
Now tug at our heart,
Tighten the cords around our chest and throat.

The no-moreness of it all . . .
No more the anticipation of that birth,
No more joy beside that sweet, sweet crib,
No more around the table, gathering,
No more tedious, 'just one more'
    bedtime request,
No more driving for scouts or sports,
No more the phone that constantly rings,
No more arguments, the 'being needed,'
No more the dreams,
No more a future for our child.

Wherever we were in that growing stage,
The stage is now dark.
Only the emptiness of your absence,
Only the dull despair of these early days.

Yet change does come.
Goldenrod and purple aster and yellow leaves.
Mellow sunlight of early fall,
Embrace our senses, if we notice them at all.

Change comes more slowly
   to our hearts and lives.
It comes with the love
   of friends who listen,
It comes after exploring
   memories and feelings,
   over and over and over again,
It comes, unexpectedly,
   when we see anew . . .
It comes with re-engagement
   with needy others,
It comes as a bird-song,
   a cool breeze, the beauty of a flower,
It comes, when time, used wisely,
   has elapsed.

We have changed, we will never be the same,
We could not possibly be the same.
Our child's death has irrevocably altered us.
It is our choice, what that change shall be.

We can choose depression and defeat,
We can choose and seek a ray of hope,
   and keep on seeking.
We can choose to seek to build
   a meaning from this madness,
A way to honor and remember our loved child.
To integrate that meaning and that life,
   into our own life on-going,
As a spirit that lives on, and shares that
   new found life unto the world.

Daybreak

Dawn comes later these October morns.
At first, upon the Bay, the first red glimmer
Along horizon's line,
And then the eastern sky glows crimson,
And then the Cliffs shine gold,
And then, a darkened crab boat
    silhouette upon the sparkled waters.
It gladdens e'n my heavy heart.

And then my thoughts return
    to that horizon far,
And the poem often quoted
About the unseen . . .
    beyond what can be seen . . .
And so my thoughts go
    back and forth,
        back and forth,
In so many ways . . .

After all these years . . .
At first so full of shock and disbelief,
And then the pain, and hurt,
Of your not being with us . . .
The cutting off, of future
    hopes and dreams
        that every parent knows . . .
The slow, slow days, and weeks, and months,
That turn to years of missing you . . .

Sometimes, an artist's canvas,
The sounds of special music,

A voice that tunes its understanding,
A writer gives a gift of words . . . opens up
   a way not seen before . . .
And I dissolve in thankfulness.

For some, there is the comfort of God's presence,
For others, bitter darkness fills the night.
Where is the one who cometh to console,
To fold the soul forsaken . . .
               in overwhelming Love?
When comes the time of opening once again?
The time when trust can live again?
How cold that void!
How frozen is that heart!

And now the sun is higher,
Its golden light upon Bay
   waters more diffuse.
Now I receive its warmth,
   its beauty, its daily hope.
I feel surrounded by a Light
   that is eternal . . .

Seen, or unseen, always there . . .
Reflected from the beauty
   in the face of a friend,
   in the smallest flower,
   in the brightest leaf,
And from the unseen,
   Beyond the horizon . . .

Seasons

The season changes.
Imperceptibly, yet suddenly,
    golden leaves flutter to the ground.
Summer flowers have turned to
    autumn's mums;
Goldenrod covers the fallow fields;
In a wink, the corn stands brown.

My life changes.
In this dry time of loss
In this aftermath of my child's death,
All that went before
    is seen through a now different lens.

It is all different.
    The days are different.
        my thoughts race on in
        a confusion of unreality.
        my thoughts are on a string,
        pulled by an unknown player.
        my body held taught as a wire
        or suddenly, a mush of jelly.

Relationships are different,
Husband and wife
    each in their cocoon of grief
    flail to establish some symmetry,
    to understand the other
    in the midst of their own torment;

To support each other
    when needs may be so different;
To reinforce and reestablish love
    in this new testing time.

Then our friends are different.
Some are there with warmth and comfort,
    others seem far off,
    or demand we fit their timetable.
Their absence or abuse disturbs us
    as we dimly recognise
    they know not how to care.

We are changed now,
    Never ask when we will
        be back to normal!
    In this slow mourning process
        we will be changed forever.
    We must discover
        a new 'normal' for ourselves.
    Hesitatingly, painfully,
        building this 'new' normal.

Out of the ashes of our grief
Out of the days of our mourning,
We call to the profound depths of our being
We search for new hope.
We stir sparks from the ashes of our lives,
    here and there, a faint breeze
    creates a small flame
    to light a new way.

These changes are a melding
   of who we have been,
   of our love for our child,
   of the life and the death of our child:
All my memories, the pain, the joy,
That somewhere along this new journey
   come together
   light a flame
   sear the soul
   refine the spirit
   create a new wholeness
   undergird our 'new' normal.

The harvest moon
Slips its red-gold splendour
   over the Bay waters,
Lifts its beauty and its light across the heavens,
We have a hope of our own;
   for beauty and light
     once more in our own lives!

Change

The wind blows from the Bay,
The crabber hauls in the season's pots,
Squirrels with fat cheeks hide their nuts,
I see it all . . . un-seeing.

No longer the heat of summer,
Dead leaves now litter the grass,
No longer thoughts of Fall change,
I am now living a life so changed.

Child of my joy and my hopes,
Lies under that sad, sweet grass,
It is all so unbelievable . . .
my child, my future, now dead.

At first the days pass in a daze,
Only one thing, only one thing,
In my thoughts . . .
    It can't be true . . .
        It is true . . .
My child whom I love.

More weeks and months go by,
Do you know it is a shell that you see?
Inside is a terrible battle,
Great confusion, a feeling of grey.

Will there ever again be joy,
Aliveness within that shell?
Will I ever know another being
Who knows the things I now know?

Once, in a great museum,
I saw a great artist's work,
    "Guernica," they said,
I saw a Mother holding her dead child,
        screaming!!

My heart leapt into that Mother's heart,
And gave thanks to that great artist,
Who somehow knew the things I knew,
Yet could still draw in the farthest corner
    one small flower!

One small flower, in a painting,
Planted seeds of hope again
Learning how to nourish that wee seed,
To beautify again my world.

To see again, with a new see-ing,
Both the ugly and the pure,
To know deeply, that both are very real,
To know where I must stand.

These things my child has taught me,
My child, with whom I walk now
    in ways so changed,
And yet so meaningful,
    Together, loving the world!

The
Holidays

The Holidays
. . . for the First Time . . .
Again.

The daylight now is so much shorter,
Windows closed, curtains drawn
   against the dark
The furnace mutters in the basement.

Outside, the air is smoky in the dusk.
The final brilliance of leaves
Upon fall's bright green carpet.

At first, I think of other years,
The laughter and the innocence.
Now I can only think of "might have beens . . ."

The holidays are coming one by one:
Halloween, Veterans Day, Thanksgiving,
   Hanukkah, Christmas . . .
So many thoughts, so much ambiguity.

For weeks we see the spooky costumes.
Will we ever be so light-hearted again?
For others who have suffered violence,
Halloween may come with stunning fearfulness.

For some whose children went to war,
Veterans Day can break the heart . . .
The flag hangs down like a great tear . . .
From constricting bands within our chest.

What shall we do with Thanksgiving?
Thanksgiving for so much pain?
At first our thoughts are only of our loss,
How can it not be so?
This day of family, friends and feasting,
The absence stronger than a presence.
Let me say . . . please let me say . . . that name!

Then comes the lights of Hanukkah,
Dedicated to the Holy through millennia.
My way seems dark . . .
O let light shine . . .
(and as I wrote those words, the sun came red
from Bay's horizon, and I was warmed by
Creation's faithfulness).

And last comes Christmas,
Before the year is o'er.
What threads of love,
    remembrance, family,
Shall be woven into
    this year's tapestry?

Let us take it day by day,
As feeling and as memories arise,
Let us stay close to family,
Even when they grieve so very
    differently from us,
That we may wonder if they
    cared and loved as much.

Let us speak that name,
So loved, so painful now . . .
Yet needing to be claimed by memory . . .
Even midst this greatest hurt.
My child . . . my child . . . my child!

My child . . .
    Creation's spirit,
        Embodied through parental love.

A gift of life,
    and love,
        from Life Eternal!

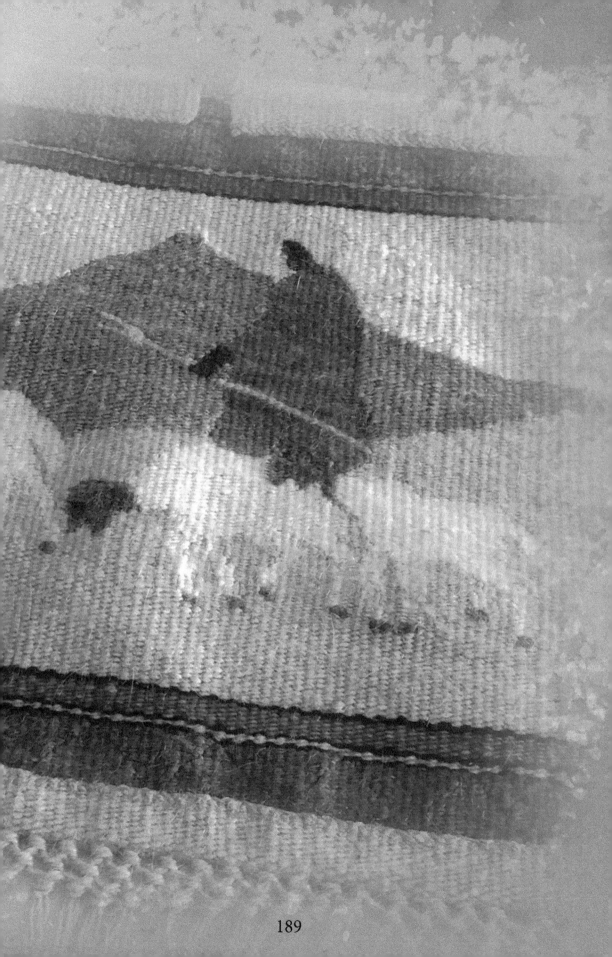

Thanks . . . Giving

The old oak tree stands by the side of the road. As its leaves gradually turn russet, then brown, then fall, its trunk and branches now outline its form. Its great round trunk sinks heavily into the earth at one end, and reaches skyward at the other. In between, gnarled branches or healed and knotty rings where former branches once grew, cover the trunk. It is a tree of strength rather than beauty; under its branches generations of children have congregated and played and been protected; it has endured much yet still stands; by this very endurance it has achieved a deeper, resonating beauty and by its wounds it imparts a sense of steadfastness, of permanence and indestructibility.

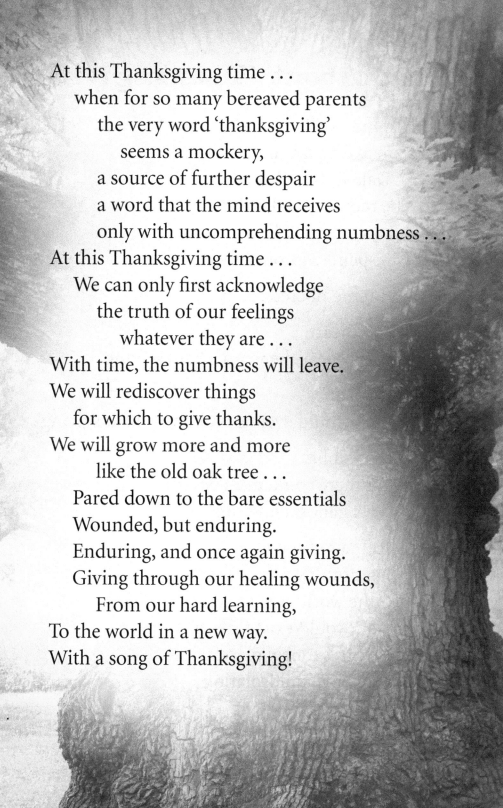

At this Thanksgiving time . . .
      when for so many bereaved parents
            the very word 'thanksgiving'
                  seems a mockery,
            a source of further despair
            a word that the mind receives
            only with uncomprehending numbness . . .
At this Thanksgiving time . . .
      We can only first acknowledge
            the truth of our feelings
                  whatever they are . . .
With time, the numbness will leave.
We will rediscover things
      for which to give thanks.
We will grow more and more
            like the old oak tree . . .
      Pared down to the bare essentials
      Wounded, but enduring.
      Enduring, and once again giving.
      Giving through our healing wounds,
            From our hard learning,
To the world in a new way.
With a song of Thanksgiving!

What About 'Thanksgiving?'

A 'friend' wrote . . .
"I am asking for him,
 . . . Dale Eugene Mondell . . .
to be remembered, this first
Thanksgiving and Christmas
I will spend without him . . ."

and I remembered . . .

my cold heart
    when I hear the word Thanksgiving

my despair
    that I would ever again know Thanksgiving

my incredulity
    that there could even be
        a Thanksgiving this year

my feelings at the deepest level
    that nothing was the same
        the world was upside down
        and I would exist forever
            in this lonely place
            of pain and isolation.

Then a 'friend' said . . .
All these feelings are normal!
I know they were not normal for me!

Slowly, I began to understand
that these are the feelings
of normal grief . . .

Grief . . .
    formerly a word
    read or listened to occasionally
    then quickly cast aside
    with a flick of the mind.
        We all want to be a stranger to grief.

But now it is thrust upon me
    and it is somehow comforting to know
        that in the scheme of grief's ways
I am normal.

Normal in an alien world
but nevertheless;
normal in this place I now find myself.

And I know a small upbeat of heart
    and am surprised
    by a sudden quickening of thanks . . . giving
for a 'friend' who shared
    that information of
    what is now normal.

And then I acknowledged that
    in this new grieving time
I have known
    the kindness of a friend
    the caring of a friend
    the sharing of a friend.
And like a miracle
I now know a glimmer of . . . thanksgiving!

First Year
Thanks . . . Giving

Those words...
   are beginning to come up:
"The Holidays"

To think of Thanksgiving
   in the first year of my loss
     is a mockery!

I am numb and void
   at such a thought . . .
I am wild with rage
   at such a thought . . .
I am in deep despair
   because it seems that never again
   will there be, in my being,
   a spark of thanksgiving . . .
I might even think
   that it could be disloyal
     to my child
   to think of "thanksgiving"

What can I do with this hurt,
   this emptiness
   this cold feeling that never again
   will thanksgiving be in my heart?

Remember well . . .
   that someone who "knows" . . .
   who has been there,
   in that first year,
   can now look back, and say . . .

195

"It does get better . . ."
    even though not as fast
    as we so desperately desire.
it is O.K. to be sad
It is necessary to accept and work
    through the pain . . .
    to acknowledge this deep distress
    to allow the tears to flow
    to ask the *why's* and *if only's*
    (though we may never find the answer)

It is also necessary
    to do the things that must be done . . .
    to find the balance between grieving
       and doing . . .
    Both are necessary!

It does help to ponder on our life,
    and on our child's life;
    to speak of our child
       to those who will listen;
    to remember the glad things
       and the bad things
       of those years . . .

It does help our surviving siblings
    if we model . . .
    that it is O.K. to cry;
    to continue to speak of the sibling;
    to laugh again;
    to know that there will be good days
       and not good days;

to recall the memories of both
the good and the not so good
and to let those memories
bring up old emotions
and then let go of those that hurt.

It does help to know that
it is O.K. to let go . . .
and to just
let be . . .

In this acceptance
is born
the memories that sustain . . .
the memories that renew . . .
the memories that become integrated within
and bring healing.

So, in this hard, tough first year
and the other hard, tough years . . .
Look for the soft wings of hope.
If they are not to be found yet,
remember that others have walked this way
and have found hope,
and so HOPE the HOPE
that you, too,
will find HOPE
and know HEALING
and murmur 'THANKS . . . GIVING'.

Changes

This is the season of change . . .

Light fades early and arrives late,
Days tremble from cool to warm
Air floats among dry leaves
as breezes bare knuckle branches.
Green turns yellow, rust and red,
as golden light shimmers across
   uncomprehending eyes.
A great sigh bursts forth:
How can there be this beauty
   amongst these day of pain?
How can the orderliness of the seasons exist
   with the unraveling of my heart?

My changes are within and without . . .

No more the midnight nursing of
   that sweet one . . .
No more the whining requests of the young
   child at bedtime . . .
No more the feel of small arms
   around my neck . . .
No more the door opening and then
   slamming shut . . .
No more the request
   for one more cookie . . .
No more the excitement of the team game . . .
   or the bright expectancy of holiday treats . . .
No more the request to use the car and the
   oft times waiting anxiety of the late hours . . .

No more the talk of proms, careers,
    or weddings . . .
No more the dreams of grandchildren
    and the maturing of our child . . .
No more . . .

These losses leave me numb and void.
Will I ever feel within myself
    a wholeness once again?

The seasons change intuitively;
Change has been thrust upon me
    as a robber of dreams . . .

Yet I slowly see
That there are other changes up to me.
I can choose some changes that will make
The present and the days ahead more fruitful.

I will walk down the grieving path
    as fully as I can . . .
I will allow my feelings
    to be expressed the best I can . . .
I will remember what the wishes of
    my child would be for me . . .
I will walk forward with the changes that
    will fill my life again . . .

So,
    changed forever,
        with new understanding
            deeper love
                and great Thanks-giving!

Holiday Thoughts

I hear the sounds of tinkling bells,
Smell the cookies baking,
See wondrous trees with shining lights . . .
And feel the tears roll down my cheeks.

I see the faces of children glowing,
Signs of the season everywhere,
Carols in the frosted air . . .
A cold weight in my heart.

In the malls the busy throngs,
Anticipation all around,
Tinsel, baubles, laughter, song,
In my throat a lump of grief.

Sometimes for a short sweet while,
I'll catch the joy of yesteryear.
When innocence and love and life
Were the only things I knew.

Before the death of my child so loved,
Before the knowledge of such sadness,
Before the
   might have beens
      the *why's*
When you were still amongst us.

How many holiday years must pass,
Before, for me, again will shine.
The tree all lighted and bedecked
With ornaments and scented.

How many days and months and years
To reach a place of my heart's ease,
To bring into that lonely place,
The memories that bring new grace?

Unto a soul that lives bereft
Unto a soul where love has slept.
When will be a new awakening
Where once again my soul will sing?

May that time soon come for each of us
When that longing does come true,
Not in ways as former known,
Yet at a deeper level, new sown.

In this soul new love revealed,
Understanding, compassion now unveiled.
A heart more open to all others
Is somehow what your life engendered.

So, ring out bells in the starry night,
Send out songs to the heavenly height,
And here on earth, let a candle's light
Reflect great love for you . . .
    my child beloved!

Sounds of the Season

Sounds of the season permeate the air.
The happy chatter of a thousand shoppers;
The voices of the children
      excited and expectant;
The music in the malls and on the radio;
The choirs singing praise and adoration;
The bells pealing in the frosted air.

We hear them...
      sometimes muffled through our fog;
      sometimes stridently and incongruently
        invading our sorrow.

Whatever they once meant,
      now all is changed.
No longer are we the light-hearted shopper;
The children's voices remind us of a new
      silence;
The music cuts our saddened heart;
The singing choirs may only add
      a discord in our search for meaning;
The bells' peal open our great despair.

What can we do with this new season,
With these sounds that leaden our soul?
Easy answers do not come.

Only the slow passing of the days and months;
Only the acknowledgment of our grief;
Only the mourning that invites others to share,
To be the friends who listen, who care.

Slowly we reach out . . . sometimes to withdraw;
Slowly we think the thoughts of our loss;
Slowly we feel the depth of our pain;
Slowly we understand
    that good mem'ries remain.

Eagerly we share words of our child
    and the name;
Eagerly we listen as others name the name;
Eagerly the remembrance embraces our heart;
Eagerly say "thanks"
    when another shares our pain.

Sometime will come a day when once again
We are the happy shopper, seeking gifts;
We hear the voice of children, and know joy;
We find feet and motion moving to the
    music's beat;
The voices of the choir now once again,
    move our being in great joy and adoration;
The bells peal in the frosted air;
And Peace of starlit skies light up our soul.

Remembrance of our child has grown within
To fill our heart with thankfulness and love,
And deep within we sing a song
To the one we now include in grateful memory.

So let the bells peal out!
Let music fill our ears!
And a great symphony of sound
Bring now a Joy which may include some tears.
And we know a peace that passeth understanding!

The Holidays

The Holidays are coming soon,
   with celebration of a Birth!
   with celebration of a Light!
     My heart feels like a heavy stone.

The sights and sounds of revelry
   of presents, trees and gladness 'round,
Come screaming in the thickening walls
   to a heart where sadness alone is found.

Now I must search within that heart
   to find a spark within that gloom,
   to hear again, and see anew,
Something of wonder . . .
Something called hope . . .

It may be just an ordinary thing . . .
   A bird in flight, red wings aflame,
   The moonlight's trail upon the Bay,
A tree that suddenly is not the same.

The 'tree' brings dreams of wonder
   of star filled skies so clear and cold
of places in the mountain or the north woods
    where silently green life and beauty grow.

The tree brings shouts of joy
   from children as they gaze
at this tree so full of lights
   and trinkets busy hands have made;

and every heart that looks
    is stirred by hope and mystery
remembering often dreams
    from days long past.

When the dreaming and the living
    sometimes feels so far apart,
to burn the smallest candle lights a way
    and hope warms hearts where
        coldness has held sway.

And when the loved ones gather round the tree
    included with the children and adults
are all the generations held
    in gentle memory
whose lives are woven strand by strand
    within our own.

O tree of soft and wondrous beauty
    may your light burn white
        within my heart;
    that Love may touch each thought
        and action that I take . . .
and Peace of starlit north woods shine . . .
    on those who gather round the tree,
        and in our memory.

Searching . . .

Music is all around,
    melodies of anticipation and of joy.
        and my heart is crying . . .

At the office, they talk of their plans
    for the holidays,
        a stone lies hard in my chest . . .

Store windows beckon hurrying feet,
    my walk is slow and hesitant,
        a tight lump binds in my throat . . .
Lights are everywhere
    except in my hollow eyes
        a well for tears . . . shed or unshed.

Over and over my mind asks . . .
    How can I be so alone?
    so cold, so heavy, so sad?
    Will this hurt ever end?
Is there someone who can understand?
Who can listen to my dammed-up cry?
What will have meaning now?
Now that my child has died?

Where is beauty?
And the place of love?
In this dull grieving time.

And I remember,
   over long intervals . . .
      a first crocus in the wet snow
      the sun's warmth at noontime
      the wind's music in the pinewoods
      the star's light upon Bay waters
      the Compassionate Friend
         who looked into my eyes
         and enfolded me with love . . .

And now I know . . .
   but oh, so slowly,
      through the grief . . .
   that hope is True
   that Love bears all
      and
         Is All.

O! Starry Night!

And now, O heart,
It is the time of
Hanukkah and Christmas.

All around I see and hear
Reminders of the Season . . .
How will I survive the season?

The music, bells, and twinkling lights,
menorah, candles, Christmas trees,
The laughter of other children.
The screaming absence in my own heart.

On leaden feet I do the things that I must do.
With choking throat I swallow
The overwhelming thoughts of you!

And then, one frosted night,
I looked up, into the sky,
Through branches bare of leaves,
And saw a starry canopy . . .

My thoughts lifted up beyond . . .
Where they'd been mired . . .
And I beheld the beauty of the heavens . . .
The never ending lights of a trillion suns.

Against the dark they glistened
Beckoning me . . .
To a place of peace . . .
A seamless universe of movement
        and of light . . .

Where estrangement is no more . . .
Where . . . what was . . . what is . . .
what is to be . . . are merged,
And dance upon a starry night!

And now I know what
I will do this Season . . .

I'll pluck those stars, and
String them on a tree, as lights . . .
I'll place them in a menorah,
     one by one . . .
I'll hang them above a cradle,
     in a manger . . .
I'll light one as a candle for
     my child, so loved . . .

And somehow, from the deepest
     longing of my being,
Arises, wondrously, a flame of hope,
Encompassing this wounded heart
     With a Peace . . .
          that passeth understanding!

This Holiday Season

I hear the sounds of this new season:
Music on the airwaves, in the malls,
Chatter of excited children's voices,
Resonance of church bells in
    canyon streets and villages.

    Yet many times I hear it not at all.
    Encased in a dark cocoon of grief,
    Oblivious to outer happenings
    Hearing only sounds of inner sobbing . . .

I smell the trees, evergreens,
Wrapped tightly on the truck,
Coming from some distant woods,
Now unfolded, breathing out
    their fragrance in crisp air.

    Sometimes I cannot allow
        myself to look
    At the things that formerly brought joy.
    The dissonance of feelings
    Reverberates so painfully within.

I see the faces, everywhere,
Responding to the magic of the season;
Softer, kinder, so expectant,
As they tenderly embrace these days.

    My heart is held in hard, tight bands,
    And within, a chilling void.
    I seem not to have the energy or will
    To step into the spirit of these days.

I wonder at the lights
Twinkling in the windows, everywhere.
The stars shine in the darkness overhead,
What does it mean . . . ?

> At first, there is a dullness
> in my soul. It shrivels.
> Is it too gone forever?
> The old words of comfort seek new meaning,
> And I despair of finding it again.

And then I saw the pine cone,
Its seeds dropped into earth,
New roots sprouting now to claim the soil
That energizes, and brings life anew.

And then I saw the faces
Of those who cared about me . . .
Articulate or inarticulate with words,
Yet caring, caring, caring . . .
And love was in my heart again.

And then I saw that star,
Shining somehow just on me,
And beaming its clear light
into my soul, to nourish its great need!

And, at last,
my cold heart was warmed,
and uttered a Thanksgiving!

Star ... Light

Outside the window
Across the dark expanse of Bay
the eye at last sees a small glimmer;
A shape takes form.
A sliver of light, pale as silver
    gleams in the deep dark;
and finally now,
    the eye looks up
    to behold a star.
What star is this?
    On a cold hillside
    in a far city
    shines on a dark granite stone;
    illuminating the chiseled letters
    of a beloved name.
    The heart reads the words
    underneath that name
    cut twenty years ago.
'Away in the ever closing night,
    thrashes again the sun.'
He wrote those words
    now shining in that starlit granite.
A heart ponders
    the mystery of love
    retold across the centuries ...
Shine on, bright star,
Your wonders to unfold
Unto a broken heart!
Look ... look for a birth!

The Gifted Tree

For those of us who travel
To Route 4 in Southern Calvert
The time has come,
The time has come again!

Going north, a new star appears,
low on the horizon, just above a barn,
In December's early dusk.
And we wonder . . .

Going south, at first a glow of light
In winter's darkness;
Approaching, a tree now visible,
Lighted with ten thousand lights.
And we ponder . . .

More than just a tree with bulbs,
It spreads a special glow
Of beauty and of mystery,
Far beyond its branches,

And in my heart and mind,
An answering response
Brings thoughts of another gift;
Of a new birth, both then, and now.

A gift is given, unconditionally,
For all to see its beauty;
We can choose to magnify the gift . . . or not.
But oh! what a difference that gift can make!

Thank you, neighbor, for your wondrous gift!

My Son
John Michael Andrews

born July 26, 1945, Australia   died April 30, 1967, Vietnam

Lived 1947 to 1966, Dayton, Ohio

This book would not have been written without the living and the dying of my first born son, John Michael Andrews. It was his death that gave me the experience to write these poems that appeared on the cover of The Compassionate Friends Calvert County Chapter's monthly newsletter from 1988 through 1995.

Michael was born in Brisbane, Australia in 1945 after my marriage to Lt. John Stewart Andrews. He lived in Dayton, Ohio with his three brothers and a sister until graduating from Colonel White High School. Then he attended Miami University in Oxford, Ohio for his freshman and first semester of his sophomore year. During that time he was active in the school's literary magazine, "Dimensions," and became its editor.

He volunteered for the U.S. Army Air Corps, became a helicopter pilot and was sent to Bien Hoa Air Force Base in Vietnam. During the three months before his death in a fiery crash of two helicopters flying on mission, he saw and wrote about what he was seeing, flying low over the land or dropping off or picking up soldiers being sent on mission on that land. His poem "Evening at Bien Hoa AFB" arrived in our Dayton mailbox three days before a military team came to our front door to inform us of Michael's death on April 30, 1967.

Marie Louise Andrews, 7.11.2020

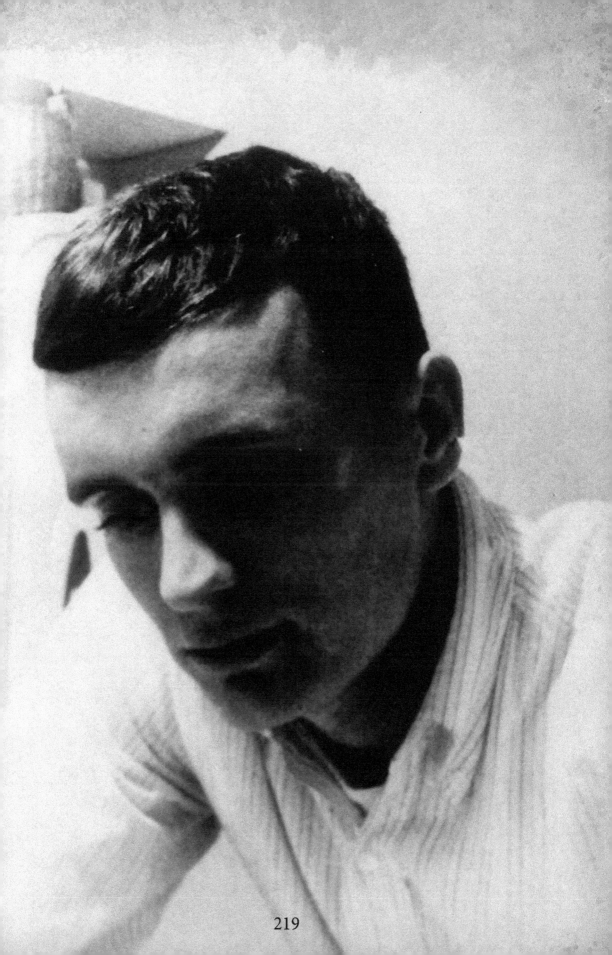

Mike's Poem

Evening at Bien Hoa AFB

I saw the Dutchman's brown today,
heard a basketball on pavement,
a Polish lady pluck some strings,
watched a ceiling fan turn slowly.

Once, I couldn't see the glimmer,
in the gloom of Rembrandt's brown,
Through my door, looking East at dusk,
I couldn't see the orange sun.

But I saw the paling sky, a
couple of darkened clouds that seemed
the shade of that dark air that wrapped
itself in folds around a mill.

A basketball seems out of place
yet someone bounces one in the
courtyard outside my door. Such sound
punctuates the quiet evening.

That deft hand disturbs the Polish
lady's music. Once, thirty years
ago she played her harpsichord
for a machine, her shoulders hunched.

Now I hear her, amid bounces.
German convolutions flash those
intricacies that dust motes swirl
wildly about the ceiling fan.

I saw the Dutchman's brown today
heard a basketball on pavement,
a Polish lady pluck some strings,
watched a ceiling fan turn slowly.

John Michael Andrews

photo credits

Page 10: "Portrait of Marie Louise Andrews." °

Page 12: "Windy Bay." *

Page 14: "Winter." *

Page 16: "Forest in Winter." *

Page 18: "Winter Morning." *

Page 24: "Silhouettes of trunk and limb." *

Page 28: "Snow Covered Woodland." *

Page 30: "My heart lies heavy." *

Page 35: "Spring Snowdrop Flowers in a Forest." Photo by Brilliance Stock, www.shutterstock.com.

Page 38: "Ice Flows, Red Sunrise on the Chesapeake Bay." °

Page 40: "A pond gleams silently." *

Page 42: "A heart can lie cold and sad and broken." *

Page 44: "Down by the Bay, the scene is monochrome." *

Page 46: "Red Hearts are Everywhere." *

Page 49: "Pencil Pine, Walls of Jerusalem National Park, Tasmania." Photo by Peter Dombrovskis, copyright courtesy of Liz Dombrovskis.

Page 53: "Family Portrait." °

Page 54: "Boy with Snowman." °

Page 56: "Beautiful Yellow Mountain Flower Breaking the Snow Cover." Photo by Mila Drumeva, www.shutterstock.com.

Page 58: "Buttercups," by spline_x, www.shutterstock.com.

Page 60: "Along the Way." *

Page 62: "Spring Cherry Blossoms at the Tidal Basin." *

Page 64: "Springtime." ° *

Page 66: "Dawn." *

Page 68: "Silent markers on the ground." *

Page 72: "On Father's Day." °

Page 74: "Small Yellow Flower in the Rain." Photo by Krys Vladimir, www.shutterstock.com.

Page 80: "Blossoms on still dark tree branches." *

Page 83: "In Waterfall Valley, Cradle Mountain Lake, St. Clair National Park, Tasmania." Photo by Peter Dombrovskis, copyright courtesy of Liz Dombrovskis.

Page 84: "New Bouquet." °

Page 86: "A Walk in the Garden." *

Page 88: "Hydrangea." *

Page 91: "Family Walking a Dog on a Beach." Photo by fizkes,www.shutterstock.com.

Page 93: "Mother Embracing Little Daughter." Photo by Altrendo Images, www.shutterstock.com.

Page 194: "Thanksgiving Celebration Tradition." Photo by Rawpixels.com, www.shutterstock.com

Page 200: "Wondrous trees with shining lights." *

Page 202: "Mother and Children Shopping for Christmas Ornaments,"
Photo by FamVeld, www.shutterstock.com.

Page 204: "Christmas Scene with Tree Gifts and Fire in the Background."
Photo by Sandra Cunningham, www.shutterstock.com.

Page 206: "Burning Candle and Christmas Decoration."
Photo by Smileus, www.shutterstock.com.

Page 208: "Crocuses on Snow." Photo by Volkova Irina, www.shutterstock.com

Page 210: "Menorah with Candles for Hanukkah on the Background of the New Year Tree." Photo
by alex_gor, www.shutterstock.com.

Page 212: "Christmas Tree Sale at Night." Photo by Checubus, www.shutterstock.com.

Page 214: "A Bethlehem illuminated by the Christmas Star of Christ; Elements of image furnished
by NASA." Photo collage by Real ICG Animation Studio, www.shutterstock.com.

Page 216: "Mrs. Weems' Christmas Tree." Painting from the Route 4 Series by Suzanne Shelden. *

Page 218: "John Michael Andrews." °

Page 220: "Scent of Maui." Photo by Danny Braddix, Jr. °

All Shutterstock imagery is licensed according to the Standard Licensing Agreement as found on
www.shutterstock.com, August 2020.

° Courtesy of Marie Andrews and family.

* Photo (unless otherwise noted) and collage work by Suzanne Shelden, Shelden Studios.

CPSIA information can be obtained
at www.ICGtesting.com
Printed in the USA
LVHW060754011220
672994LV00005B/45